REVELATION SERIES FOR ADULTS

Uniting Against Evil

Ephesians

A Study Guide
by Dale Cooper

CRC PUBLICATIONS
Grand Rapids, Michigan

Scripture quotations in this publication are from the HOLY BIBLE, NEW INTERNATIONAL VERSION, © 1973, 1978, 1984, International Bible Society. Used by permission of Zondervan Bible Publishers.

Revelation Series is published by CRC Publications,
2850 Kalamazoo Ave. SE, Grand Rapids, MI 49560.
1-800-333-8300 (US), 1-800-263-4252 (CAN).

Library of Congress Cataloging-in-Publication Data
Cooper, Dale, 1941-
Ephesians: uniting against evil: a study guide / by Dale Cooper.
p. cm. — (Revelation series)
ISBN 1-56212-223-1
1. Bible. N.T. Ephesians—Study and teaching. I. Title. II. Series.
BS2695.5.C66 1996
227'.5'0071—dc21 96-46428
CIP

10 9 8 7 6 5 4 3 2 1

Contents

Leader's guides and other study guides may be ordered by writing CRC Publications at 2850 Kalamazoo Ave. SE, Grand Rapids, MI 49560, or by calling toll-free 1-800-333-8300 (US) or 1-800-263-4252 (CAN). Please refer to the following product numbers as needed: Leader's Guide, #1310-0440R; Study Guide, #1310-0400R.

Introduction

"Here's the way it is, and here's what you can do." With this simple strategy Paul undertakes the enormous task of motivating beleaguered believers in Christ "to keep the unity of the Spirit" so that they can "live a life of love" (Eph. 4:3; 5:2).

Never mind that these dear friends of Paul are half an empire away in the region of Ephesus, struggling under the fist of Rome and, worse, under the onslaughts of the evil ruler whose kingdom is "the air" (2:2). Never mind that Paul can't visit his friends but can only write them a letter because he's a prisoner in Rome (3:1; 4:1; 6:20).

None of that ultimately matters because God loves all of them and has chosen them from eternity in Christ to be his adopted children (1:4-5). And Christ, who now sits at the right hand of God "far above all rule and authority" (1:21), has redeemed all of them "through his blood" (1:7), whether Jews or Gentiles, making them "God's people and members of God's household" (2:19) and thus opening the way to "the riches of his glorious inheritance" (1:18). What's more, God strengthens all of them "with power through his Spirit" so that Christ may live in their hearts "through faith" (3:16-17). And by that power they can "grasp" and experience the vast love of this God "who is able to do immeasurably more than all [they] ask or imagine" (3:18-20).

With that (and much more), in roughly the first half of his letter, Paul lays out for his dear friends "the way it is," encouraging them with praise upon praise about who God is and what God has done for them. And in the rest of the letter Paul spells out what his Christian friends "can do" (not on their own, but) in the "incomparably great power" (1:19) of God in Christ through the Holy Spirit.

They can "live a life worthy of the calling [they] have received" (4:1): to be the church, the body of Christ (1:22-23), making God's salvation known throughout the cosmos (3:10). They can unite together in the Spirit, using the gifts God gives them to build each other up toward maturity (4:3, 12-13, 16) and to submit to one another in love, following Christ's example (5:1-2, 21)—and they *must* do these things in God's love and power if they are to fend off the attacks of the devil, that evil "ruler . . . of the air" (2:2; 6:11)! Equipped with "the armor of God" and praying "in the Spirit on all occasions," they can "stand firm" (6:11, 14, 18) "to the praise of [God's] glory" (1:14).

As Paul encourages and builds up his Christian friends, we hear him speaking to us too. We hope this study of Ephesians is encouraging and upbuilding to you.

The Education, Worship, and
Evangelism Department of the
Christian Reformed Church

Rev. Dale Cooper, chaplain at Calvin College, Grand Rapids, Michigan, has written this study guide. An accompanying leader's guide written by Rev. Kenneth A. Baker, a Christian Reformed pastor in Kalamazoo, Michigan, includes helpful background material and suggestions for leading the discussion of each lesson.

1 From Eternity, for All Things, Forever

Ephesians 1:1-10

[1]Paul, an apostle of Christ Jesus by the will of God,

To the saints in Ephesus, the faithful in Christ Jesus:

[2]Grace and peace to you from God our Father and the Lord Jesus Christ.

[3]Praise be to the God and Father of our Lord Jesus Christ, who has blessed us in the heavenly realms with every spiritual blessing in Christ. [4]For he chose us in him before the creation of the world to be holy and blameless in his sight. In love [5]he predestined us to be adopted as his sons through Jesus Christ, in accordance with his pleasure and will—[6]to the praise of his glorious grace, which he has freely given us in the One he loves. [7]In him we have redemption through his blood, the forgiveness of sins, in accordance with the riches of God's grace [8]that he lavished on us with all wisdom and understanding. [9]And he made known to us the mystery of his will according to his good pleasure, which he purposed in Christ, [10]to be put into effect when the times will have reached their fulfillment—to bring all things in heaven and on earth together under one head, even Christ.

Try to imagine the scene, for it actually happened. Pope Gregory I, the great church leader serving as spiritual father to Christians throughout the Western world from A.D. 590-604, receives a letter from an elderly, faithful Christian woman. She's troubled about her sins and wonders whether she can really be sure that Jesus loves her.

The humble woman asks the venerable church leader, simply and directly, "Can I know, beyond doubt, that Jesus is my Savior and that he will love me forever?" The pope's response: "Yes, for sure." Then she writes another letter, asking, "How?" The response: "You must believe that he is your Savior from your sins, *and* you must do good and righteous things for him to show that you love him." In her third letter the woman asks, "What kinds of things? And how many?" The pope replies, "You can do a whole variety of things to show Jesus your love. You can pray, give to the poor, show mercy, worship, be kind . . . lots of things. And how many? Well, you can always do more, of course. . . ." In her final letter the woman asks again, "Holy Father, if I can—and must—always do more, then can I *really* be sure Jesus loves me?" The pope's answer: "You can be *almost* sure."

In for a Treat

This woman's searching questions and the pope's answers are a fine place for us to begin our study of Ephesians. For these vexing issues are with us still, and Paul's letter, soaked richly in spiritual insight and direction, addresses them. Every chapter of this letter—virtually every sentence—is cool water to parched heads and hearts, nourishing food for hungering souls. Continually in this letter Paul talks about "the riches of God's grace" (Eph. 1:7), which are presented to us "in Christ." Paul encourages his readers—and us—to receive these riches so that "we will in all things grow up into him who is the Head, that is Christ" (4:15), and to "be filled to the measure of all the fullness of God" (3:19).

Ephesians is chock-full of keywords that demarcate the very contours of the gospel message. Paul refers to "glory" four times; "grace" eleven times; "fullness," "fills," and "filled" six times; and—the font of all these riches—"in Christ" fourteen times. Studying these chapters, savoring these immense truths, we're sure to be in for a treat. My prayer—I trust yours too—is that God's Spirit will use what we do together to bring each of us closer to "unity in the faith and in the knowledge of the Son of God . . . attaining to the whole measure of the fullness of Christ" (4:13). In the first several lessons (covering Eph. 1-3) we'll focus (as Paul does) on what God has done for us in Christ; then we'll follow Paul's lead as he lays out for his readers what these teachings mean for living the Christian life together as God's people. One of the strongest and most important themes in this letter of Paul is *unity,* for believers need each other, empowered by the Holy Spirit for God's glory, to resist the sinful nature and the devil's attacks and to grow into the Spirit-led community God intends them to be.

An Apostle . . . to the Saints

Few things in life are more exciting—and few positions more privileged and honored—than to be the first to announce an important piece of good news.

God is actively pursuing a grand and vital work in this broken, tired world vandalized by trouble and sorrow, discord and death. The divine rescue effort is as wide and deep and high and long as the reach of the entire cosmos and is infinitely more pervasive than the sin that so pitiably damages all that's good in God's creation. God's goal is nothing less than "to bring all things in heaven and on earth together under one head, even Christ" (1:10). And Paul, by the will of this very God, has the privilege of announcing this good news. Paul is an "apostle," a person sent on a mission.

When Paul wrote this letter of Ephesians, he was in prison in Rome (3:1; 4:1; 6:20), probably about to pay with his life for his devotion to his calling. But by no means does he consider himself a victim of unfortunate circumstances or shoved around willy-nilly by some supposed fate. On the contrary, his mood is buoyant and radiant, and his outlook for the future is confident. In a way far deeper and more penetrating than what appeared on the surface of events, God was at work in the very heart of history, and Paul, as herald, was participating in the overthrow of evil.

Paul begins his letter by wishing his readers "Grace and peace" amid the troubling circumstances that he and they were in the midst of. The phrase is anything but a meaningless formality. "Grace" (*charis*) is one of the richest words in the New Testament, identified with the word "joy" (*chara*). It means "the spring and source of joy," and Paul used it as a shorthand term to denote all the riches that Christ's gospel brings. "Peace," too, is anything but an empty formality. For Paul and the early Christians this word brought to mind the Hebrew sense of *shalom,* the delightful "singing together" of the entire creation, as God originally intended it, in true justice and wonderful delight. Where the creation flourishes, *shalom* is at work. By wishing his readers "grace and peace," then, Paul is longing for his friends to have the very best in life, the deep and lasting joy and peace that God in Christ can bring. For they—and he—are "saints," holy people set apart by God to become more and more like Jesus Christ, God's own firstborn Son.

Chosen in Christ

In verse 4 Paul begins a torrent of words that gushes forth to verse 14—these ten verses make up one sentence in the original Greek text. But only grammarians protest. Paul was being swept away with delirious joy as he tried to shape into words what wonderful things the holy and good God had done for his people through Jesus Christ.

Paul's words are nothing short of stupendous. He stretches way back beyond time to eternity itself and says that, yes, already then God was thinking about his people, loving them, and planning every exquisite detail of their deliverance and new life in Christ. Of course, what Paul is teaching here extends far beyond the capacities of our feeble minds to embrace. But to him two facts are clear: (1) his own sick, sad, and sinful past is proof that we are all dead in our sins; and (2) our salvation is nothing hastily thought up or contrived as some stopgap measure to counteract human sin. Rather, from eternity itself God has chosen us and loved us. The initiative for our salvation therefore lies with God, not with us.

Awe, rather than reason, is the only appropriate response to the wonder-filled mystery of our election in Christ. So in praise to God we sing,

'Tis not that I did choose Thee,
For, Lord, that could not be;
This heart would still refuse Thee,
Hadst Thou not chosen me.

Thou from the sin that stained me
Hast cleansed and set me free;
Of old Thou hast ordained me,
That I should live to Thee.

To Our Lord's Greater Glory

Why did God take pains to accomplish this electing and saving work on our behalf? For one final and singular purpose: so that we, with all the rest of creation, might enhance God's glory and sing of his grace (1:6, 12). Sun, moon and stars; turtles, tarantulas, and tulips—yes, "all creatures, great and small"—join in chorus to sing their Maker's praise (see Ps. 19). Even Jesus, God's firstborn Son, came to earth to bring back glory to his Father in heaven (John 17:4). We human beings, too, the apex of all that God has made, must now, with our rebel fists unclenched, lift our hands in praise. Someone once said that to be human is to be one point in the universe where God's goodness can and should receive a corresponding echo of gratitude for what the Lord has done. (See also Deut. 26:19; Isa. 43:7, 21; 62:7; Jer. 13:11.)

Redemption by His Blood

Not wishing to interrupt what he's thinking and saying, Paul continues by stating that God's work of electing and saving us has been achieved at unbelievable cost to himself. God redeemed our lives through the death of his very own Son.

"To redeem" is a concept rich in meaning. Both Jewish and Gentile readers likely caught the world-shaking significance of what Paul is claiming here, for *redemption* (*agorazo, exagorazo, luo*) has its analogs both in the Old Testament and in the ancient pagan world. The Jews had their Old Testament "kinsman redeemer," one who recovered a poverty-stricken relative's property rights by paying that person's debt (see Ruth 3-4). And in the customs of ancient pagan warfare, vanquished high-ranking officials who were taken captive could be bought back and set free by their fellow citizens for a ransom—a redemption—paid to the victors.

As sinners, says Paul, we are no longer free people. Because we have turned away from God through our sin, we are enslaved to our sinful nature. But Christ has redeemed us; he has paid the price required by God "to fulfill all righteousness" for our sake (Matt. 3:15). In this way Christ has opened the way for us to be reconciled with God (2 Cor. 5:15-21; Col. 1:20). When we remember this, our lips inevitably sing forth praise: "Oh, for a thousand tongues to sing my great Redeemer's praise."

When Jesus came to redeem his people, a new era began to burst onto the scene. What excited Paul and ignited his entire passion was this compelling vision: "all things in heaven and on earth" (Eph. 1:10)—not less than *everything* God has made—are to be brought together and completed in Jesus Christ. Adam's sinning separated us from community with God in paradise; Christ's redemption recovered that blessed relationship for us. Jesus, our Savior, is the very center of history. When Paul thought again and again about what God through Christ had done for him and, yes, for the entire cosmos, he knew that only one response was appropriate: "I consider my life worth nothing to me, if only . . . [to] complete the task the Lord Jesus has given me—the task of testifying to the gospel of God's grace" (Acts 20:24).

General Discussion

1. No sooner has Paul given his readers the loaded greeting "Grace and peace to you . . ." than he launches into a soaring praise song to "the God and Father of our Lord Jesus Christ." Why? What has Paul got to sing about here? What effect might such an opening have on his readers?
2. What does it mean to be "blessed . . . in the heavenly realms with every spiritual blessing"? (Eph. 1:3). Make a list of the spiritual blessings you have, and share one or two of these items with your group.

3. When it comes to being certain about your salvation, is Ephesians 1:4-6 reassuring to you? Explain. Do you have any problem with the teaching of these verses? Explain.
4. Suppose someone curious about Christianity asked you, "What is God doing in the world, anyway?" How would you answer? Compare your answer with Ephesians 1:10. What evidence do you see that God is making progress in bringing "all things . . . together under . . . Christ"?
5. Why is God's revelation called a "mystery"? (Eph. 1:9-10; see also Col. 1:25-29). To whom has God made this "mystery" known? What are the implications of this revelation for the church? What relevance does this revelation have in our North American culture today?

Ideas for Small Groups

Opening (5-10 minutes)

Pray/Worship—Open your first session of this study of Ephesians with a prayer for God's wisdom and guidance as you look to the Scriptures to grow and mature in faith. Thank God for bringing your group together for this Bible study, and since part of this session's focus is on praise, consider singing together an opening praise song in worship of the Lord, who blesses us so richly. For example, right after the prayer you could sing "Father, I Adore You," "Praise to the Lord, the Almighty," "We Will Glorify the King of Kings," or another praise song your group members know well.

Share—If your group is used to meeting together, you'll want to take some time to catch up on how things have been going since you last met. If some or all of you haven't been part of this group before, you'll want to introduce yourselves and perhaps each share something about yourself that you'd like the others in the group to know. For starters, you may want to share with each other the expectations you have as you begin this study of *Ephesians: Uniting Against Evil.*

Focus—The focus question in each lesson is designed to get you thinking about the lesson material and how it affects you. Ask yourself the following focus question as you begin this session: *What does God's grace in Christ mean to me?*

Growing (35-50 minutes)

Read (Optional)

You may want to read Ephesians 1:1-10 together (as well as the study-guide notes) before moving into a discussion time.

Discuss

Before choosing from among the following process questions for your discussion, you and your group will want to work through some of the "General Discussion" questions, choosing especially from questions 1-4, which relate well to the questions that follow.

On grace, peace, praise, and blessing:

- What have you learned about "grace and peace" in this lesson?
- List the spiritual blessings you find in Ephesians 1:1-10. In what ways do these blessings inspire you to praise God in Christ?
- What can you do to help God bring about more peace and blessing in your personal life? In your small group?

Goalsetting (5 minutes)

Try to work on the following goal in the coming week:

- Here's what I want to do to help God bring about more peace and blessing in my personal life:

Closing (5-10 minutes)

Preparing for Prayer

This is a time for sharing praise items and concerns that you'd like the others in your group to bring before God in prayer for you, both now and during the coming week. You may also want to ask for prayers for God's help in meeting the goal you've set during this session, or perhaps in addressing a specific need in your spiritual life, family relationships, or another area.

Prayer

Close your meeting with prayer, asking the Lord to help you live lives of praise and service for his glory. Group members may join in with their prayer concerns and praises. Then ask for God's blessing and guidance in the coming weeks as you study more about the book of Ephesians together, seeking to learn and grow in faith. Before you part till your next meeting, join in singing together, if you like, a simple familiar praise song such as "King of Kings and Lord of Lords" or "Praise God, from Whom All Blessings Flow."

Group Study Project (Optional)

As a result of studying Ephesians 1:1-10, some or all of you may wish to learn more about grace and living gratefully for God. Explore your local library or bookstore and see what you can come up with. One of the newer books we can recommend on this topic is *The Riddle of Grace* by Scott Hoezee (Eerdmans, 1996). Perhaps you could report on your findings when you meet to discuss lesson 3, "A New Creation—by Grace." As you work on this study project, try to highlight, for the group's benefit, how the author relates grace to our living in unity as God's people.

2 Sealed with God's Spirit, Called to Hope in Christ

Ephesians 1:11-23

[11]In him we were also chosen, having
been predestined according to the plan of
him who works out everything in conformi-
ty with the purpose of his will, [12]in order
that we, who were the first to hope in
Christ, might be for the praise of his glory.
[13]And you also were included in Christ when
you heard the word of truth, the gospel of
your salvation. Having believed, you were
marked in him with a seal, the promised
Holy Spirit, [14]who is a deposit guaranteeing
our inheritance until the redemption of
those who are God's possession—to the
praise of his glory.

[15]For this reason, ever since I heard about
your faith in the Lord Jesus and your love for
all the saints, [16]I have not stopped giving
thanks for you, remembering you in my
prayers. [17]I keep asking that the God of our
Lord Jesus Christ, the glorious Father, may
give you the Spirit of wisdom and revelation,
so that you may know him better. [18]I pray
also that the eyes of your heart may be
enlightened in order that you may know the
hope to which he has called you, the riches
of his glorious inheritance in the saints, [19]and
his incomparably great power for us who
believe. That power is like the working of his
mighty strength, [20]which he exerted in
Christ when he raised him from the dead
and seated him at his right hand in the
heavenly realms, [21]far above all rule and
authority, power and dominion, and every
title that can be given, not only in the
present age but also in the one to come.
[22]And God placed all things under his feet
and appointed him to be head over
everything for the church, [23]which is his
body, the fullness of him who fills every-
thing in every way.

People tend toward one of two reactions as they think about their future: either they dread it and become paralyzed, or, standing on tiptoe, they are eager and "can't wait" for the future to happen.

Faithful Christians need not be anxious, says Paul; in fact, they must daily be ready and eager as they greet the future. They must live in hope. *For the favorite tense of the Bible is not the past and not even the present but the future.* For Christians, the best is yet to come.

Our Spiritual Inheritance

History, of course, deals with past, present, and future, and from beginning to end the Bible proclaims that the hottest piece of news is what the one history-making God has been doing in it. God has been deliberately active in all of history, working out "everything in conformity with the purpose of his will" (Eph. 1:11). Everything!

This profound, sweeping claim calls for meditating—deep, careful, Spirit-led pondering that can vitally transform the way we view our life situations. No detail of my life, your life, or anyone else's escapes God's sovereign attention and control. Every circumstance serves as malleable clay for God to use in shaping us into persons of higher holiness.

Note the grand sweep of divine activity in the lives of all who belong to God. God "chose us" (1:5, 11) and determined to save us according to a purposeful, established plan. God's purposes for all creation are in no way willy-nilly, some divine "afterthought," so to speak. Quite the contrary. The one almighty God has a purpose for his creation and for each person who belongs to him. And that purpose is vitally linked to Christ, God's firstborn Son, through whose death and resurrection God has set about accomplishing it.

And why has God been ceaselessly at work in history to accomplish this purpose? Simply stated: "in order that we . . . might be for the praise of his glory" (1:12, 14). God, who is central in everything, has made and remade us for his glory. Our single pursuit, as Jesus reminds us, must be to live in such a way that we bring glory to our Father in heaven (Matt. 5:13-16). What a dramatic, arresting thought for a twentieth-century generation of self-maximizers, who sometimes stupidly suppose and act as though all of life and history ought to revolve around them!

In salvation history the Lord set about methodically to bring his people home again. God first chose the Jews, who therefore became "the first to hope in Christ" (Eph. 1:12). Paul was among these Jews and, with others, he heralded the good news of salvation to them first (Acts 11:19; Rom. 1:16). But later he and others proclaimed the same message to the Gentiles, who "also were included in Christ when [they] heard the word of truth, the gospel of . . . salvation" (Eph. 1:13). Now all people, both Jews and Gentiles together, share in the same inheritance.

Sealed with the Holy Spirit

What God began to do through Jesus Christ is now continued through the Holy Spirit, who applies Christ's work to every believer. The goal for everyone who belongs to God is clear: each one must come to know God better (1:17). And the Holy Spirit is presently at work in each believer's heart to accomplish this goal. The "you" in 1:13 is emphatic, not referring to humanity in general but to specific people: believers in Christ. Paul adds the word "also" to indicate that the Spirit's grand activity takes place not just among a few select believers—some early Jews, say, or a few of Paul's original readers and listeners. No, the Holy Spirit is at work in every single believer, applying Jesus' work and bringing us to fuller maturity as God's people.

In this work the Holy Spirit functions as a "seal" for our benefit (1:13; see also 4:30). Seals accomplish three purposes: to attest that a work is genuine and authentic; to signify ownership; and to lock up a container and make its contents secure. Each of these purposes is important for us in relation to the Holy Spirit. First, the Spirit verifies that we are God's called-out children. When our hearts become weak and our souls become so tired that we wonder whether God's promises are true and whether we are in the embrace of his love, the Spirit shores us up and continues to supply peace and power to our distraught and frantic souls.

Second, the Spirit attests that we belong to no one else but God, that we are indeed "God's possession" (1:14). When we, vulnerable as we are to Satan's lures and lies, become tempted to imagine that we belong to someone or something other than God—say, the corporation we work for, the nation we live in, or some other created entity—then the Holy Spirit calls us back and reminds us who we really are and to whom we really belong. We are God's—and God's alone.

Third, the Spirit makes us secure forever. The Greek word *arrabon* in 1:14, in reference to the Spirit, means "installment, pledge, deposit." The Spirit, then, is God's down payment, so to speak, verifying that God will continue the work begun in us until the final day of "redemption of those who are God's possession" (1:14). The Spirit is our daily assurance, amid all the twists and turns of our tattered and often tragic lives, that God will see us through. God's Spirit will lead us—*home!*

A Warm and Unceasing Prayer

The transitional phrase "For this reason" (1:15) links the grand theological themes Paul has been discussing with what is to follow. He now offers a prayer of thanksgiving for his Christian brothers and sisters for the way they have been putting their trust in Jesus and showing their love not just for one another but for "all the saints."

Grand theology is important, to be sure. Exploring the depths of biblical teachings is important, for neglecting to do so is certain to make believers hungry and eventually to let them starve. But, important as theology is, it is also insufficient. Good theological thinking must eventually give proper shape to practical living. The ultimate test of any theological teaching lies in its ability to be applied to one's life. It ought to lead us to greater trust in Jesus as Savior and Lord and to greater and deeper love for fellow believers. And this is not to be some narrow affection for a select group of believers, a few who think "like we do" or who belong to our denomination (or some faction within it). No, it's to be a love "for all the saints" (1:15), as Paul clearly states.

Paul's prayer for his readers also includes a plea. He "keep[s] asking" the sovereign "God of our Lord Jesus Christ" to supply "the Spirit of wisdom and revelation" so that the Ephesian believers may come to know God better and better (1:17). A person will never come to know Jesus as Savior and Lord by merely "trying real hard" to believe. To believe in God and to grow in the knowledge of God requires first a dependence upon the Lord and his Spirit, who initiates faith and maintains it in the believer's heart.

Paul pleads further that the "eyes" of his readers' "heart may be enlightened" to know hope (1:18). Paul is referring to the heart here as the center of one's being, the seat of one's will, one's knowledge, one's understanding. For it's in the heart that the "Spirit of wisdom and revelation" comes to live in order to enlighten and transform a person through and through. So Paul's plea is that his Ephesian brothers and sisters will continue growing in the knowledge of God so that they can hope in the Lord with all their heart, so that they can have a lively hope in God and in all God's promises for their future. Day by day they can grow more confident as they face their future in Christ—and thus be less paralyzed by fear—so that they can continue living for him in "love for all the saints" (1:15).

Now, the hope Paul is speaking about here is not some vague crossing-one's-fingers-hope-against-hope that things might turn out all right. Rather, it's anchored in the very actions of God in history, including the sure promise that God is completing what has already begun in Christ.

Jesus, History's Absolute Lord

With that sure hope in mind, Paul concludes this part of his letter with a breathtaking recital of what God has done through Jesus Christ, highlighting Christ's absolute supremacy over all of history. Raised by God from the dead, Jesus is now seated in honor at God's right hand, exalted "far above all rule and authority, power and dominion, and every title that can be given, not only in the present age, but also in the age to come" (1:21). (See also Matt. 28:19-20.)

Further, Jesus wields his awesome power for the welfare of those who belong to him. He's the "head over everything for the [sake of his] church," and the church, "his body," is the awesome "fullness of him who fills everything in every way" (1:22-23). What a rich relationship between Christ and his church!

As believers, we need never fear about the present status of our Savior and Lord, nor of our security in him. As the Heidelberg Catechism says, in God's care "we can be patient when things go against us, thankful when things go well, and for the future we can have good confidence" (Q&A 28). Because of all God has done in Christ for us, we can live—and love—for him in Christian hope.

"He's got the whole world in his hands"—and each of us as well.

General Discussion

1. You may have noticed that in our Scripture for this lesson Paul moves from declaring God's praises (Eph. 1:11-14) to asking God for more blessings (1:15-23). What's the connection between these activities? Further, what's the connection between "grand theology" and practical living? In each case, what effect would it have on your life if you were preoccupied with one over the other?
2. Today it is increasingly common for individuals and churches as well as companies to write "mission statements" that indicate their sense of calling or purpose. How might Ephesians 1:11-12 influence your personal mission statement? How might 1:13-14 influence your church's mission statement?
3. In Ephesians 1:18-19 Paul prays for spiritual enlightenment that will raise his readers' awareness about three matters: "hope," "riches," and "power." What difference

would each of these make for your (personal) faith and for the church's faith today if you (and the church at large) grew in these areas?

4. How is the church ordinarily portrayed in our society today? Give examples from books, movies, documentaries, news media, politics, and so on. Compare these examples with the portrayal we find in Ephesians 1:22-23. What difference should this biblical teaching make for our sense of mission in the world?

Ideas for Small Groups

Opening (5-10 minutes)

Pray—Open your session with prayer, asking for the Lord's presence in your hearts as you study about the importance of the Holy Spirit and our hope in Christ.

Share—Share with each other how you're doing with the goals you set in lesson 1.

Focus—Ask yourselves the following focus question as you begin this session: *What is the extent of my hope in Christ?*

Growing (35-50 minutes)

Read (Optional)

You may want to read Ephesians 1:11-23 together (along with the study-guide notes) before moving into your discussion time.

Discuss

Before choosing from among the following process questions for your discussion, you'll want to work through some of the "General Discussion" questions, especially questions 3 and 4, which focus on our hope and power in Christ.

On the Spirit and our hope and power in Christ:

- In this lesson what have you learned about being sealed with the Holy Spirit?
- How does this knowledge about the Holy Spirit affect your hope in Christ?
- In what ways can you put this hope to work for Christ in your personal life? In the work of the church?
- How much power do you believe is available to you in Christ to be a part of his mission in this world?

Goalsetting (5 minutes)

Try working toward the following goal in the coming week:

- I want to grow in my sense of hope through Christ's Spirit, and here's how I would like to put that hope to work, in Christ's power:

Closing (5-10 minutes)

Preparing for Prayer

Share items that you'd like the others in your group to bring before God in prayer for you, both now and during the coming week. You may want to mention personal concerns and praises, the goals you've set so far in this Bible study, and so on.

Prayer

Close your meeting with prayer, thanking God for the seal of the Holy Spirit and the hope we can have to live forever in the power of Christ. Everyone may join in with their prayer concerns and praises. Before parting till your next meeting, you could add a worship element by singing together any combination of the following songs about the Spirit of Christ and his power to help us live for him in hope: "Spirit of the Living God," "Dwell in Me, O Blessed Spirit," "O Worship the King," and "From Ocean unto Ocean."

3 A New Creation—by Grace

Ephesians 2:1-10

[1]As for you, you were dead in your
transgressions and sins, [2]in which you used
to live when you followed the ways of this
world and of the ruler of the kingdom of the
air, the spirit who is now at work in those
who are disobedient. [3]All of us also lived
among them at one time, gratifying the
cravings of our sinful nature and following
its desires and thoughts. Like the rest, we
were by nature objects of wrath. [4]But
because of his great love for us, God, who is
rich in mercy, [5]made us alive with Christ
even when we were dead in transgressions—
it is by grace you have been saved. [6]And God
raised us up with Christ and seated us with
him in the heavenly realms in Christ Jesus,
[7]in order that in the coming ages he might
show the incomparable riches of his grace,
expressed in his kindness to us in Christ
Jesus. [8]For it is by grace you have been saved,
through faith—and this not from your-
selves, it is the gift of God—[9]not by works,
so that no one can boast. [10]For we are God's
workmanship, created in Christ Jesus to do
good works, which God prepared in
advance for us to do.

Three sobering, arresting memories spring to mind as I reflect on this passage:

- Some time ago a college junior acknowledged to me his long pattern of alcohol use. Gradually he had become addicted. He had begun drinking in seventh grade, and by tenth grade he was totally hooked. "I tried and tried to quit," he lamented, "but I found myself powerless to do anything about it. My will was as drunk as I was." To "Just Say No" was for him no longer possible.
- A young man, caught up in a pattern of deceit, lying, and flagrant lawbreaking, was arrested and wrote to me one of the most depressing letters I have ever received. Penitent for what he had done and remorseful for all the pain he had inflicted upon so many of his family and friends, he cried out, "I have lost so much because of the terrible things I have done. I find myself screaming Psalm 51 every night. Does God hear me through my endless tears and sobbing? Chaplain Cooper, I am sorry. I do not write for your sympathy—in fact, I don't want any sympathy. I don't even want to send this letter. As I look back and reread it, I ask myself why I even wrote it. Lord Jesus Christ, have mercy upon me, a miserable sinner."
- G. K. Chesterton once said that the Christian teaching about sin and evil does not even require faith—it is provable by evidential data.

The Human Morass of Sin and Evil

Throughout history people have had varying estimates about our ability as humans to live together politely and well, to be moral, and to create a just and good society. Some scholars, their optimism unchecked, claim that in our heart of hearts we human beings really are good. "I'm OK—You're OK," they say, "so in our dealings with one another let's show on the outside what we are on the inside. When we do that, we'll craft an OK society, quite free of the niggling troubles and imperfections that have vexed us in the past."

These optimists are willing to concede that, of course, none of us is perfect. Not yet. We're still crippled by several factors: ignorance, stupidity, and a bad environment. Until now these factors have limited our ability to act well. But we humans, say the optimists, now have the capacity in ourselves to correct these flaws: by education we can remedy ignorance; through selective human breeding we can get rid of the stupidity brought on by genetic defects; and by tidying up our neighborhoods we can put everyone in a better frame of mind to do what's right and fitting.

The apostle Paul is a lot less hopeful about the human prospect. His grammar in Ephesians 2:1-3 may be wrenchingly difficult—in the original text there is no subject or verb until verse 4—but what he's saying about us human beings is unmistakably clear: at the very core of our existence we are not nice people. In fact, we're evil through and through—Paul's word for us is *nekros*: we're "dead"; we're like corpses walking around. And we're in desperate straits because of the sin that thoroughly pervades each one of us. No matter how well we've mastered, how high we've risen to establish our fame and prestige, we are still in a dreadful state. The sickest and most vile among us are those who, trying to hide from themselves and to deceive others, put on the thin jacket of respectability and pretend they're not like others.

Paul says that we once "followed the ways of this world" (Eph. 2:2). In the original Greek text the verb for "followed" means literally "to walk around" (*peripateo*), and it's a favorite metaphor of both Paul and John in the New Testament. No less than thirty-two times—eight of them in Ephesians—they use this verb to describe the day-to-day pattern of one's ordinary living. *Peripateo* can be used to describe the regular, often unspectacular, but steady progress of a redeemed person trying to live by the promises and commands of God (see Eph. 4:1; Rom. 6:4). This verb can also describe the habits of unredeemed people who live "according to the flesh," or "by the standards of this world," that is, disobediently (see 1 Cor. 3:3; 2 Cor. 10:2). Paul's point here is that every believer, prior to God's rescue, once lived by the pattern, the principles, and the motives of "this world" (*kosmou toutou*). We were continually seduced by its evils, and we fell prey to its sickly impulses and enticements.

We followed the "ruler of the kingdom of the air" (Eph. 2:2). The Greek word for ruler (*archonta*) denotes "one who is chief, first, highest." And the phrase "the kingdom of the air" refers to the popular idea in those days that while the gods were in heaven and humans were on earth, the air in between was inhabited by spirits, some of them evil. Paul refers to this common notion to remind his readers that they were held captive to evil influences and spirits before Christ came to free them.

Continually "gratifying the cravings of our sinful nature and following its desires and thoughts," we became "by nature objects of wrath" (2:3). Note how in this verse Paul turns from "you" to "we": he includes himself in the miserable plight in which all humans find themselves. Duped by the evil one and enslaved by lustful cravings from which we *could not* free ourselves even if we wished to—"My will was as drunk as I was"—we received our due consequence: the wrath of God.

Talk today about God expressing anger and wrath toward human beings, and most people will raise their eyebrows, as if to say, "You can't be serious! A God of wrath!?" After all, God in his very nature is one who loves and is merciful. How can he display something so hostile as wrath?

The Greek word for wrath (*orge, orgao*) literally means "to teem, to abound, to swell (with moisture) as it ripens, to become passionate and excited." So what Paul is saying here is that the consistent, regular, and patterned wrongdoing of human beings has evoked a predictable, consistent, and intensifying response within God. The Lord has become swollen with anger toward his creatures and is now full of ripened wrath. In God there is nothing out of character, fanatical, or arbitrary in this matter. Our continual human evil has simply gradually increased the furious heat of God's anger. Further, it's important to know that along with being loving and merciful, God is also holy. This means the Lord is wholly opposed to evil; evil has no place or standing in the presence of the one holy God. One day God will unleash his furious wrath on all evil, but for the time being, out of love and mercy, God is holding back that wrath so that we may repent and seek forgiveness and new life through Christ. (See Col. 1:21-23; 2 Pet. 3:9; Rev. 16-20.)

We human beings cannot begin to gauge the magnificence of God's amazing love until we begin to visualize, through the eyes of faith, the full blast of God's white-hot displeasure and anger against all our wrongdoing. Eliminate sin from human conversation nowadays, and we'll eventually also do away with grace. Discard the teaching about God's furious wrath (against evil), and we will also do away with the splendor of divine forgiveness.

The seventeenth-century Puritans, careful about cultivating godliness, made it a habit to think daily about some things in life that really matter. Here is the tenth item from Richard Rogers's list of "Twenty Profitable Subjects for All to Meditate Upon": "whether we have not bestowed some time not only in mourning for our own sins, but also for the sins of the times and age wherein we live." Wise people don't slight sin. They pay attention to it.

"But . . . God . . ."

What a dramatic, arresting interruption Paul makes to his sobering litany of the mess we have made in our human sin: "But God . . ." (Eph. 2:4, RSV)! Says Martyn Lloyd-Jones: "These two words, in and of themselves, in a sense contain the whole of the Gospel." When our situation was bleak and utterly hopeless, God, in Christ, did for us what we could never do for ourselves: he saved us (2:5; Rom. 5:6-8). God's intervention has made all the difference.

What has God done for us? Three things: "made us alive *with* Christ" (Eph. 2:5), "raised us up *with* Christ," and "seated us *with* him in the heavenly realms" (2:6).

Note the bold and daring claims Paul is making here about the present status of believers, those rescued by God. Paul is saying that Christ is not only *for* us, but he is also *with* us, and we are *with* him!

Again and again throughout his letters Paul underscores the close relationship between believers and their Lord. The apostle generously sprinkles favorite phrases such as "in the Lord," "in Christ," "in him," and so on—no fewer than 164 times. Here, now, Paul uses the preposition "with" to indicate the unbreakable bond between Christ and those who belong to him. We have been resurrected with Christ, we now have a new life with him, and we have even already begun to reign with him.

Contrary to some present hymnody that tends to emphasize that our triumph with Christ is still far-off and coming, Paul says that salvation for us is *now.* It has already begun. Jesus, having completed his saving work on the cross and now seated at the right hand of honor and power with his Father in heaven, has seated us there with himself! The coming age, in which we shall live with Christ and reign with him forever, is only a fuller and more intense continuation of what has already begun. In Christ and by the power of the Holy Spirit we can begin to enjoy and exercise our "spiritual [salvation] blessings" even now (1:3). Just one example of this is the power we can have, by the Holy Spirit, to let go of our worries and stop trying to run things in our own lives so that God can use us for his purposes—right where we are. (See Matt. 5:25-35; Phil. 4:12-13.)

Why has God done all of this for us? Paul uses four phrases here, each of which describes God's very nature and clarifies God's motive. God has "great love for us," is "rich in mercy" toward us (Eph. 2:4), shows us "the incomparable riches of his grace," and has expressed his "kindness to us" (2:7). Our sin and God's resulting anger toward us never have the last word in the relationship the Lord maintains with us. God the Judge has become our Father. When our claim to his mercy and love was fully spent, God—inexplicably and quite beyond our ability to understand—loved us by grace alone.

Someone once asked Karl Barth, one of this century's greatest theologians, what was the deepest and most compelling truth he had ever discovered and explored. His answer, as simple as profound, was, "Jesus loves me, this I know."

Wise people today, in addition to meditating on their sin and evil, do well, says the Puritan Richard Rogers, to daily "cherish our faith by taking comfort and great delight in the great benefit of our redemption by Christ." How often during the day don't we need—truly—to meditate intently upon the amazing grace of God that saves wretches like us!

God's Workmanship

As if to build toward a crescendo, Paul stunningly reverses the word order in 2:10 (in the Greek text), placing heavy emphasis on the last word of this phrase as follows: "For of him we are a workmanship." (Most English translations follow this pattern.) The word translated as "workmanship" is *poiema.* From it we derive our word *poem.* Paul declares, in effect, "Behold, what a specimen of divine poetry each of us really is—sheer artistry, a masterpiece!" In other writings, as in this verse, Paul describes us as newly "created in Christ Jesus" (2:10; see 2 Cor. 5:17; Gal. 6:15)—each one of us who believes in Christ!

In my work as a pastor among college-age young people, I hear no more frequent and recurring refrains than these: "I'm not really worth very much"; "I don't think very much of myself"; "Who cares about me?"; "What am I good for?" Lack of a proper self-esteem nowadays is epidemic.

The solution to the problem is not to be found in fighting one's way toward looking good—dieting, exercising to stay in shape, dressing fashionably. Nor in fighting to prove oneself smarter—high grades, entrance into a top graduate school, landing a fine job. Nor in money—having high income, driving sporty cars, flaunting what one has acquired. Nor in power—shoving one's weight around, wielding influence over others. People who attempt to establish their identity and secure their worthwhileness by their own power and ability eventually become tired and weary. And they lose whenever someone sharper, smarter, or more influential comes along.

The key to proper self-esteem lies here: *We are God's masterpiece,* originally made by the one God and Creator of all, and now remade in Christ. We are loved, accepted, forgiven, and made secure forever. And all because God has been, now is, and forever will be so very good to us.

General Discussion

1. Many North Americans today believe that education is the solution to such social problems as AIDS, teen pregnancy, drug and alcohol abuse, and racism. The assumption is that "to know better is to do better." In the light of Ephesians 2:1-10, how would you evaluate such a conviction, and what would you offer as a Christian alternative?
2. On the basis of Ephesians 2:1-5, in what way is the notion of "free will" a myth? How might these verses affect the way that you pray about your (and the church's) witness to people who are spiritually lost?
3. The notes above suggest that "wise people don't slight sin. They pay attention to it." How do we (or should we) "pay attention" to sin in our lives? In our worship? Is enough attention paid to sin in our church communities today? Why or why not?
4. What does it mean to you to be "made alive with Christ," "raised up with Christ," and "seated with him in the heavenly realms"? (Along with Eph. 2:4-10, see Rom. 6:1-14; Col. 3:1-4.) How does this relate to being "God's workmanship"? (Eph. 2:10).

Ideas for Small Groups

Opening (5-10 minutes)

Pray—Open with prayer, asking the God who is "rich in mercy" to guide your study about sin, grace, and our being new creatures in Christ.

Share—Share with each other how you're doing on the goals you've set in previous lessons. Perhaps now or at another time during this session any group members who have studied the topic of grace ("Group Study Project," lesson 1) could share their impressions, especially in terms of how grace relates to our unity as God's people.

Focus—Reflect on the following focus question as you begin this session: *What does being re-created in Christ mean to me?*

Growing (35-50 minutes)

Read (Optional)

You may want to read Ephesians 2:1-10 together (along with the study-guide notes) before moving into your discussion time.

Discuss

Before choosing from the following process questions for your discussion, work through some of the "General Discussion" questions, especially questions 1, 3, and 4.

On sin, grace, and new life in Christ:

- What have you learned about sin and grace in this lesson?
- In what ways do you "pay attention" to sin in your own life? In your personal worship time with God?
- What does it mean to you to have new life through grace in Christ? What can (or do) you do to show others that you have this new life?

Goalsetting (5 minutes)

Try working on the following goal as a result of this session:

- I want to apply myself to show others the new life I have in Christ. Here's what I want to do, in the strength of the Holy Spirit:

Closing (5-10 minutes)

Preparing for Prayer

Share items that you'd like the others in your group to bring before God in prayer for you.

Prayer

Close with prayer, asking God to help each one of you recognize the sin in your lives and to help you live grateful new lives in Christ. Group members may join in with their prayer concerns and praises. Before parting, you might sing worshipfully together "Love Divine, All Loves Excelling," "Lord, I Want to Be a Christian," or another familiar song about living for Christ.

Group Study/Work Project (Optional)

Perhaps your group would like to learn about and help to shape social programs and public policy from a Christian perspective. You could gather information by contacting your church's political action committee; a Christian AIDS-awareness group; Christian social-help or family-service organizations; your denomination's domestic relief organization; your local, state, or congressional representatives; or other sources. To begin, you might assign one or two group members to search out information and possibilities for the group's involvement; then at a later meeting you could review the gathered information and decide on a program, campaign, or other activity to get involved in.

Group Study Project (Optional)

Some or all of you may wish to read *Not the Way It's Supposed to Be: A Breviary of Sin* by Cornelius Plantinga, Jr. (Eerdmans, 1995), and report on its main points during a later session (such as lesson 9 or 10).

4 Hostility Erased

Ephesians 2:11-22

[11]Therefore, remember that formerly you
who are Gentiles by birth and called
"uncircumcised" by those who call them-
selves "the circumcision" (that done in the
body by the hands of men)—[12]remember
that at that time you were separate from
Christ, excluded from citizenship in Israel
and foreigners to the covenants of the
promise, without hope and without God in
the world. [13]But now in Christ Jesus you
who once were far away have been brought
near through the blood of Christ.

[14]For he himself is our peace, who has
made the two one and has destroyed the
barrier, the dividing wall of hostility, [15]by
abolishing in his flesh the law with its
commandments and regulations. His
purpose was to create in himself one new
man out of the two, thus making peace,
[16]and in this one body to reconcile both of
them to God through the cross, by which he
put to death their hostility. [17]He came and
preached peace to you who were far away
and peace to those who were near. [18]For
through him we both have access to the
Father by one Spirit.

[19]Consequently, you are no longer for-
eigners and aliens, but fellow citizens with
God's people and members of God's house-
hold, [20]built on the foundation of the
apostles and prophets, with Christ Jesus
himself as the chief cornerstone. [21]In him the
whole building is joined together and rises
to become a holy temple in the Lord. [22]And
in him you too are being built together to
become a dwelling in which God lives by his
Spirit.

Item: On a recent Larry King show a caller complimented North Carolina Senator Jesse Helms: "You should get a Nobel Peace Prize for keeping down the [six-letter racial slur] for all these years." Senator Helms replied, "Thank you."

Item: On a visit to the Indiana State Penitentiary, Mike Singletary, retired Chicago Bears linebacker—a black man—joined Chuck Colson from Prison Fellowship—a white man—to speak to the inmates. When Singletary spoke, only the blacks cheered; when Colson spoke, only the whites applauded. The inmates had segregated themselves.

Item: How often haven't we heard (or used) the derisive comment "He's just not our type," "She's not one of us," or "They're so different" (read: "inappropriate").

Is it my imagination, or is the intolerance that previously simmered beneath the surface in our society now bubbling forth? We have always had fringe groups on the left and right, but our mainstream political, religious, and social organizations have managed to remain open to accommodating others and listening to their points of view. Lately, however, it seems that society has become polarized. We seem to shout more (and more shrilly) at one another than we embrace one another.

Divisions rage both outside and within the body of Christ. We pit ourselves against one another and arm ourselves with arguments—and sometimes with weapons and terrorism—as if to get our point across. We're becoming a society of *us versus them:* women v. men, rural v. urban, black v. white, conservative v. liberal, right v. left, capitalist v. socialist, NRA v. gun control, pro-choice v. anti-abortion, gay v. straight, single v. married—the fault lines are everywhere, even within the body of Christ.

Alienation and Separation

Paul begins this section of Ephesians with "Therefore" (2:11), because what he has to say next is a direct consequence of what he has just affirmed in 2:1-10. Since everyone in Christ has been saved by God's goodness alone and each of us is God's workmanship, none of us is or may be treated as an outcast or alien—no matter who we are or what part of society we belong to. We now belong, completely and forever, to the household of God. We form the temple in which God is pleased to dwell.

Ancient society, like ours, was shot through with divisions. Free people held slaves and looked down on them as inferiors—chunks of protoplasm to do menial work. Men looked down on women and considered them inferior. Greeks cherished their Hellenist culture and deemed all others barbaric. Jews, chosen by God and set apart from other nations by the distinguishing mark of circumcision, shoved their thumbs under their armpits in pride and sneered at Gentiles, labeling them "unclean" and "uncircumcised."

Gentiles were clearly unwelcome within the inner sanctum of the Jewish temple. A wall with clear "Gentiles: No Trespassing" signs prevented them from proceeding any farther than the outer Court of the Gentiles.

But far worse than any social ostracism the Gentiles may have felt, they were spiritual outsiders, "foreigners to the covenants of the promise" (2:12). Before Jesus came, only the Jews had received the covenant of God and were his covenantal people. Gentiles had not received God's law, the priesthood, the covenant promises, and the Lord's guidance and protection (see Deut. 32.9-14). So in that sense they were "without hope and without God" (Eph. 2:12).

Signs of hopelessness were everywhere. The ancient Greek dramatist Sophocles once said, "The best thing to happen to a man is never to be born; the next best thing is to be born and die prematurely." A Roman, expressing his despair, composed this epitaph to be placed on his tomb: "There was a time when I was not; then I became; now I no longer am. I do not care." These voices have modern echoes.

We should note, however, that although the Gentiles were "foreigners to the covenants," it was always God's purpose to include them. Even in God's first covenant promise to Abraham we read, "All peoples on earth will be blessed through you" (Gen. 12:3). As we learn in Paul's next few lines, it took Christ to fulfill these words of God's promise.

The Dividing Wall Dismantled

The Gentiles, once considered "far away" (Eph. 2:13; see Isa. 57:9; Acts 2:39)—a rabbinic term of reproach toward Gentiles—"have been brought near through the blood of Christ" (Eph. 2:13). In Christ the Gentiles' spiritual alienation has come to an end. For Jesus breaks down "the dividing wall of hostility" (2:14) and restores peace among all who belong to God.

When Christ died on the cross, he abolished "in his flesh the law with its commandments and regulations" (2:15). The great wall that the Jews had erected to keep their distance from the Gentiles was the intricate system of ceremonial feasts, sacrifices, and standards of cleanliness. But all this had now come to an end; Christ has made the final sacrifice. By his death all people now have access to God's grace.

Note that Christ not only brings peace but also "*is* our peace" (2:14; see Mic. 5:5). The peace of Christ is so thorough and pervasive that it has created an entirely new community, "one new man out of the two" (Eph. 2:15). And this peace is so much more than the mere elimination of hostility. It is not simply the absence of something negative. It's *shalom*, which is far richer and more positive. My Hebrew dictionary defines it as "completeness, soundness, welfare, peace." *Shalom* is the way God intends his creation to function; it's the "flourishing of creation" with justice and delight, as Cornelius Plantinga, Jr., puts it in his book *Not the Way It's Supposed to Be.*

Paul's Jewish readers would have understood the immense depth and breadth of the term *shalom*; his Gentile readers perhaps less so. But the same Christ "came and preached" *shalom* to both (2:17).

To both Jews and Gentiles Jesus gave "access to the Father by one Spirit" (2:18). The word for "access" (*prosagoge*) occurs only three times in the New Testament, and in each instance the word refers to the believer's ready entrance into God's presence. In ancient society a *prosagogeus* was a highly placed court official who led guests into the presence of the king and introduced them to him. The *prosagogeus* brought them near and gave them the privilege of entrance. Christ does this for each and every believer, both Gentile and Jew. None has a right to come by himself or herself; only through Christ's blood and "by one Spirit" are we brought again into God's holy presence and welcomed (2:18).

Citizens, Household, Holy Temple

In 2:19-22 Paul uses three metaphors to summarize his discussion about the deep unity Christ came to bring. "Foreigners and aliens" have been transformed into *"fellow citizens"* with God's people; strangers now belong to *"God's household"* (2:19); and what were once separate, clashing, unfitting elements now have been honed to become "a *holy temple* in the Lord" (2:21).

This section of Paul's letter begins with a strong transitional phrase that means "Wherefore therefore" ("Consequently" in NIV—2:19). Paul is the only writer to use this term in the New Testament. But whenever he does, he means to strongly underscore the truth of the claim he is making. His thought here seems to be "If all that I have been explaining in verses 11-16 is true—and it most certainly is—then, as surely as night follows day, Gentiles and Jews are related to one another in a manner that is constructive, peaceable, harmonious, and utterly non-alienating to any person or group. For all of us together are now citizens of a single commonwealth, members of one family, a building in which God himself has taken up residence."

The Greek word for "city" is *polis*, and for "citizen," *polites*. A citizen was a full member of a city or state. Foreigners and aliens (*xenoi* and *paroikoi*), though permitted to live in the city and to work there, clearly were second-class. They had no protection under the law, could be expelled at any time, and had no rights of appeal. They didn't fully belong.

Now, Paul is saying that when Jesus came, he established a whole new commonwealth of subjects who reside within the boundaries of his nation and belong to him as full citizens. All of us who believe in Christ have the rights and privileges of full citizenship in this commonwealth.

But our relationship to God is even richer and more intimate than being citizens of a commonwealth. We are members of "God's household," the family of God. Jesus Christ, God's firstborn Son, and we, God's adopted children, are treated in the same manner—within the strong embrace of divine grace and love. (See also Rom. 8:15-17.)

Together, Jewish and Gentile believers now form a structure so stunning in its beauty—the church—that God is pleased to take up residence in it. The church is built on "the foundation [that is, the teachings] of the apostles and prophets." And Christ himself is the "cornerstone," the chief stone among all the stones in the entire structure, the primary anchor and foundation for all the rest.

What vivid word pictures these are to describe God's people, now gathered into a community in which the Lord is pleased to reside, with its constituent materials fitting so wonderfully together! Considering all this, how can anyone who belongs to Jesus and bears the title "Christian" even hint that another of Christ's followers doesn't really fit or belong?

General Discussion

1. How would you respond to someone who said, "We are New Testament Christians. Why do we have to sing the Psalms in church and hear sermons on the Old Testament? And why read the law if Christ has 'abolished' it?" (Eph. 2:15).
2. How do you respond to the question "Is it my imagination, or is the intolerance that previously simmered beneath the surface in our society now bubbling forth?" What divisions or hostilities do you see or experience in the Christian community today?
3. Are there barriers in your church that may prevent some newcomers or fellow members from feeling like true

"fellow citizens"? (Eph. 2:19). Give two or three examples. What can you do to help break down those barriers and promote peace and unity in Christ?

4. Reread Paul's prayer in Ephesians 1:18-19. How might Ephesians 2 contribute to the enlightenment Paul desires for his readers? Having studied both parts of Ephesians 2, do you feel motivated by what God reveals there? How and why?

Ideas for Small Groups

Opening (5-10 minutes)

Pray—Begin your meeting with a time of prayer, asking the Lord to give each of you insight into reconciliation and healing as you study about God's removal of hostilities to create a new people in Christ.

Share—Share with each other how you're doing on the goals and/or group projects you've set out to accomplish.

Focus—Keep the following question in mind as you work through this session: *What does the idea of unity in the church mean to me?*

Growing (35-50 minutes)

Read (Optional)

You may want to read Ephesians 2:11-22 and the study-guide notes together before your discussion time.

Discuss

Before choosing from the following process questions for your discussion, you'll want to work through some or all of the "General Discussion" questions, especially questions 2, 3, and 4, which focus on breaking down divisions and hostilities and uniting as God's people.

On breaking down hostilities:

- What have you learned in this lesson about God's work of breaking down hostilities through Christ?
- List a few examples of divisions and hostilities that you've seen broken (or breaking) down in your church and/or small group. How have these changes helped to bring peace and create a stronger unity?

On uniting as God's people:

- Reflect together on the images Paul uses in 2:19-22: "fellow citizens," "members of God's household," and "a holy temple in the Lord." In what way(s) do you see each of these relating to unity in Christ? What other images help you to think of God's people as a unified whole?
- What does unity do for you as a part of God's people? What do your efforts at unity do for God?

Goalsetting (5 minutes)

Try working on the following goal as a result of this session:

- With the Spirit's help, I would like to work in the following ways in my personal life so that I can help God's people grow in unity:

Closing (5-10 minutes)

Preparing for Prayer

Share items that you'd like the others in your group to bring to God in prayer for you.

Prayer

Close with prayer, asking God to help all of you see the divisions and hostilities that need to be broken down so that believers in Christ can live and serve God in peace and unity. Group members may join in with prayer concerns and praises. Before you part till your next meeting, you might invite everyone to light candles and bring them together to light a common "unity" candle while singing "We Are One in the Spirit" or another song highlighting our united life and purpose in Christ.

5 A Servant of the Gospel—by Grace

Ephesians 3:1-13

[1]For this reason I, Paul, the prisoner of
Christ Jesus for the sake of you Gentiles—
[2]Surely you have heard about the
administration of God's grace that was given
to me for you, [3]that is, the mystery made
known to me by revelation, as I have already
written briefly. [4]In reading this, then, you
will be able to understand my insight into
the mystery of Christ, [5]which was not made
known to men in other generations as it has
now been revealed by the Spirit to God's
holy apostles and prophets. [6]This mystery is
that through the gospel the Gentiles are
heirs together with Israel, members together
of one body, and sharers together in the
promise in Christ Jesus.
[7]I became a servant of this gospel by the
gift of God's grace given me through the
working of his power. [8]Although I am less
than the least of all God's people, this grace
was given me: to preach to the Gentiles the
unsearchable riches of Christ, [9]and to make
plain to everyone the administration of this
mystery, which for ages past was kept
hidden in God, who created all things. [10]His
intent was that now, through the church, the
manifold wisdom of God should be made
known to the rulers and authorities in the
heavenly realms, [11]according to his eternal
purpose which he accomplished in Christ
Jesus our Lord. [12]In him and through faith in
him we may approach God with freedom
and confidence. [13]I ask you, therefore, not to
be discouraged because of my sufferings for
you, which are your glory.

Just for fun, try diagramming some of Paul's sentences sometime. It can be a nightmare, especially when the sentence goes on and on, as in the original text for this passage, marked by the twelve verses of Ephesians 3:2-13!

Paul stops his train of thought midway through his opening sentence in this section of his letter (Eph. 3:1). Something important has come to mind, and he wishes to share it with his readers. The thought can't wait, so he sidetracks the main sentence for a while—a long while. Verse 14 marks the place where he finally comes around to it again and brings it to proper conclusion (as we'll see in lesson 6). But the material in between—3:2-13—is a parenthesis, an important parenthesis.

Paul, Christ's Prisoner for the Gentiles

The Roman heads of state, commanding a vast empire, had a big problem on their hands. They could scarcely keep the empire from flying off at the edges. The many peoples under their rule often lived hundreds of miles from Rome and were different from the Romans. The languages, religions, and customs of those peoples were extremely diverse.

To remedy the situation and to bring about at least some measure of political unity and cohesiveness in their far-flung domain, the Romans decided to make the emperor their god and to require everyone in the empire, as an act of political allegiance, to worship him.

It worked—fairly well. One headstrong people, however, the Jews, gave the Romans fits. The Jewish people so abhorred the thought of worshiping another god that they simply refused to bow down. Thus the Romans, to keep the peace, made an exception for the Jews.

When Christianity appeared on the scene, Jesus' followers laid claim to this exemption. *After all,* they argued with Rome, *aren't we Jews, and aren't the promises to Abraham, Isaac, and Jacob our promises too?* For a time the Romans, quite dull to the fine-print differences between Judaism and Christianity, extended the favor to Christians.

Eventually, however, Gentiles began streaming into the Christian company too. Then Rome determined it had had enough. It put down its strong and determined foot and demanded that every Jesus-believer must also bow down in worship to the emperor. The penalty for refusing was imprisonment, exile, even death.

Heroically the Christians stood firm. As a result, *en masse* they were often rounded up and hurled into dark prisons. However, they viewed their fate as anything but a tragedy. Instead they considered it a noble honor to bear the title of "prisoner of Christ Jesus." Paul, too, once a Christian-persecutor whose will and heart were later captured and taken prisoner by Jesus Christ (see Acts 9), was also bodily imprisoned by Rome, probably about to pay with his life for his devotion to his calling to preach Christ to the Gentiles, as we noted in lesson 1.

Paul's Mission

Many of us know—some of us firsthand—the tragic consequences of Alzheimer's disease. Over time its victims become increasingly disoriented, their memory begins to fade, and eventually they end their lives in conscious-less apathy. Though their bodies may keep going, they lose their minds totally and become oblivious to everyone and anything going on around them.

People can degenerate also into an Alzheimer's disease of the spirit. Failing, quite easily, to ask themselves regularly some vital questions—Who am I? Why am I here? Where am I going?—they begin to fill up their days with stupid frivolities and with dull, meaningless routine.

Paul, on the other hand, had a mission in life, an unflinching commitment to be a herald of Jesus Christ. He lived and breathed that mission. It charged him and got him going in the morning, and he dreamed about it at night. Read Acts 20:24—Paul's life-text, a charter for his life.

Paul didn't think up his calling by himself or nurse it into existence. Rather, it was a high and holy charge laid upon him from above, a "gift of God's grace" (Eph. 3:7; see 3:2). And it gave him a sharp and crisp answer to life's central questions: Who, why, and whither? Simply stated, Paul was a servant of Jesus mandated "to preach to the Gentiles the unsearchable riches of Christ" (3:8). This mission would consume him for the rest of his days, and he gave to it not less than everything in his being.

Why all this activity and effort, often done against considerable human resistance and in peril of losing his life? Simply this: Paul had been entrusted by God himself with heralding God's mission. From this strategic activity nothing—not even the power of the Roman sword nor the dank and dismal confines of a jail cell—could tear him away.

Paul kept his head on straight and his priorities in order while he discharged his task. He kept reminding himself—and telling others—that he himself was no big deal. He called himself "less than the least" (3:8—the original word here has a comparative ending attached to a superlative, so it literally means "leaster" or "lessermost"). Paul was well aware of the ever-present danger of becoming a celebrity. Christians may well become famous—Paul himself became very well known—but they may never allow themselves to become celebrities. For celebrities begin to believe the press reports about how good they are and how important they have become. Eventually they end up thinking themselves bigger and more significant than the task to which they have been called.

Paul ran hard and fast away from any hint of celebrity status. He makes this clear again to his readers in 3:13, saying that his sufferings are their "glory." In this way Paul comes back to his point in 3:1 and thus explains the reason for his parenthesis: to reassure his readers of his authenticity as "prisoner of Christ Jesus for the sake of you Gentiles" (3:1). Paul knew, and he wanted his readers to know, that it was God's lavish favor—grace alone (3:2, 7-8; see 2:8-9)—that had turned him into a "man with a mission."

God's Grand Purpose

Through Paul's exalted words in 3:10-11 God's Spirit permits us a brief but powerful glimpse of what the Lord is doing through the rough and tumble of human history. The one almighty God is accomplishing every one of his purposes day by day in Christ. This mighty and divine work is not always—perhaps not even usually—visible on the exterior of history's events, of course. But by faith in God one can begin to look into history's interior, into what is really happening there, and to note with awe the God who is ceaselessly at work. "Through the church" God is making his wisdom known "to the rulers and authorities in the heavenly realms" (3:10). Scholars debate over who these "rulers and authorities" are, but, as the leader's guide to this Bible study points out, it seems "more consistent with 1:21 and 6:12 to think of them as the hostile heavenly forces that stand opposed to the Lord. By this interpretation, the church stands as God's clear testimony to such powers concerning the divine plan of salvation." Always accomplishing his plans, God is guiding history home to its proper and victorious end.

God is in charge, and because of Christ we are amazingly privileged to "approach God with freedom and confidence" (3:12). Therefore, Paul encourages his readers, none who belong to Christ need ever lose heart or become utterly "discouraged" (3:13).

What a picture Paul presents in this parenthesis, this pause in his train of thought. We see a *big God* accomplishing *grand designs,* in part *through faithful heralds* who are *saved by grace* and *given the mission* to share *"the unsearchable riches of Christ"* (3:8). If we meditate on this picture for a few moments, there's no doubt that it will charge our courage and strengthen us to live day by day with the central and compelling purpose of living for God in Christ by his Holy Spirit.

Doing that, we can put the trivialities of life, its irksome and unimportant details, into their proper place—details like how long and complicated Paul's sentences sometimes are.

General Discussion

1. Paul "had a mission in life, an unflinching commitment to be a herald of Jesus Christ. . . . It charged him and got him going in the morning, and he dreamed about it at night." Do you feel a calling and desire to witness to the gospel as well? Do you observe it in your church? Why or why not? What have you learned from this Scripture passage that might renew or reinforce a passion for witness in your personal life and in the life of your church?
2. Paul refers to himself as "less than the least of all God's people" (Eph. 3:8). What does this assessment tell us about Paul's priorities? How do you account for his saying this and yet not feeling unworthy of the "high and holy charge" to serve Christ?
3. In the light of Ephesians 3:6, 10-11, how would you respond to statements like these: "I can accept Christianity, but not the church." "The church is the biggest obstacle to the spread of the gospel today."
4. In Ephesians 3:13 Paul assumes that his readers are feeling discouraged that he is in prison. Are there setbacks or disappointments in the church today that leave you feeling discouraged? What are they? How might this verse help to put those setbacks into perspective?

Ideas for Small Groups

Opening (5-10 minutes)

Pray—Begin your meeting with prayer, requesting the Lord's guidance as you study about the revelation of God's good news and the mission of serving Christ and his church.

Share—Share with each other how you're doing on the goals you've set in the past couple of lessons. Now may also be a good time to share about your progress on any group projects you may be doing.

Focus—Keep the following question in mind as you work through this session: *What does the idea of being a servant of the gospel mean to me?*

Growing (35-50 minutes)

Read (Optional)

You may want to read together the Scripture passage for this lesson (along with the study-guide notes) before moving into your discussion time.

Discuss

Before choosing from the following process questions for your discussion, you'll want to work through all of the "General Discussion" questions.

On serving Christ and his church:

- What do you think of Paul's example as a servant of the gospel?
- In what ways would you say Paul's self-image might clash with today's popular ideas of what a self-image should be?
- What's the first example that comes to mind when you think of the church's failings? Share why this example is significant to you, if you feel comfortable doing so.
- As a group, list as many positive aspects of the church as you can think of. How do these compare with the negatives people mentioned in the previous question? Who would you say is responsible for the negative aspects? For the positive ones?
- What can you do to work against the church's failings and to build up its positive points as you seek to serve Christ and his church?

Goalsetting (5 minutes)

Try working on the following goal as you seek to live for Christ:

- With God's help, I want to work against the following negative aspects of the church and build up the following positive aspects:

Closing (5-10 minutes)

Preparing for Prayer

Share items that you'd like the others in your group to bring to God in prayer for you. Mention personal concerns and praises, the goals you've set so far in this study, and so on.

Prayer

Close your meeting with prayer, asking the Spirit to empower each one of you to serve Christ and his church faithfully and with awe at the amazing God who puts purpose in our lives and is guiding history home. Everyone may join in with their prayer concerns and praises. Before parting till your next meeting, encourage each other to apply yourselves to the goal you've set as a result of this lesson.

6 An Impassioned Prayer

Ephesians 3:14-21

[14]For this reason I kneel before the Father,
[15]from whom his whole family in heaven
and on earth derives its name. [16]I pray that
out of his glorious riches he may strengthen
you with power through his Spirit in your
inner being, [17]so that Christ may dwell in
your hearts through faith. And I pray that
you, being rooted and established in love,
[18]may have power, together with all the
saints, to grasp how wide and long and high
and deep is the love of Christ, [19]and to know
this love that surpasses knowledge—that
you may be filled to the measure of all the
fullness of God.

[20]Now to him who is able to do immea-
surably more than all we ask or imagine,
according to his power that is at work within
us, [21]to him be glory in the church and in
Christ Jesus throughout all generations, for
ever and ever! Amen.

To understand what one Christian really thinks about fellow believers, check not only what she might say to them, or even to others about them. Listen also to what she prays about them. For prayer is the finest measure of a Christian's deep and sincere heart-thoughts.

Whom Paul Prays To

In Ephesians 3:14-21 Paul utters a sublime and affirming prayer to God for his beloved Christian brothers and sisters. His posture itself is special. Usually biblical people stood to pray, but here Paul falls to his knees with intense seriousness. He's about to begin a time of solemn pleading with God on behalf of his friends in the region of Ephesus.

"For this reason I kneel" (Eph. 3:14). For what reason? Paul is referring to what he had mentioned back in 2:19-22: his desire that his friends continue to be "built together to become a dwelling in which God lives by his Spirit" (v. 22). Paul longed for these believers to grow spiritually and to become together the temple in which God was pleased to reside and from which his glory would shine.

The way we view God when we pray shapes the very nature of how we pray and of what we pray for. To whom does Paul address his plea? To "the Father, from whom his whole family in heaven and on earth derives its name" (3:14-15). Paul, his Ephesian brothers and sisters, and every other group of Christians together comprise the family of God. Together we are children of a common Father, for we belong to God in Christ.

When we pray, then, we are not screaming for the attention of some distant and uncaring deity—an out-of-sorts and preoccupied being to whom our cries are a nuisance. No, we are praying to our "Father," the very One who made us, who continues to care about us, and who will never turn away from us in callous unconcern. God is delighted when we come and speak with him, especially when, as we see in Paul's example, we remember others within the family who are precious to God. Praying for his Christian friends here, Paul is confident that God will heed his heartfelt plea.

From this God, claims Paul, the entire family of believers "derives its name" (3:15). In other words, they take on God's identity and character. In the Bible one's name reflected one's nature, one's character. So the point of what Paul is saying here is that we who believe in God through faith in Jesus Christ have come to bear the very "family likeness" of God; we reflect the traits of God's own character.

What Paul Prays For

Paul's central desire for his readers, his chief request to God for them, is that they may grow spiritually. To Paul, a people's relationship with God is more important by far than anything else—financial security, respectable social status, even physical safety—that he might be able to wish for them. He's eager primarily for the spiritual welfare of his friends in Christ: "I pray that out of his glorious riches he may strengthen you with power through his Spirit in your inner being" (3:16).

What's more, Paul is aware that he's asking from a big God, the one God whose "glorious riches" for blessing are infinite and breathtaking in their splendor. So Paul is not hesitant to make a huge request on behalf of his readers: "that [God] may strengthen you with power . . . in your inner being."

To make a plea for power is to admit that we do not possess this power in ourselves. We're thus admitting that we human beings by ourselves are tired, fragile, and weak. So let's be clear: Paul is not talking here about "intending to do the best we can for God," as in "putting forth our best effort" to dedicate ourselves entirely to the Lord. Trying that, we're certain to fail every time. For our own power, however great we think it may be, is pitifully limited.

Most people limp through life using, to a greater or lesser degree, the normal strength and power available to them. Every once in a while, however, they find themselves bumping up against an obstacle that taxes their powers to the limit. Then they need extraordinary strength, a fresh and unusual burst of power from an outside unusual source. Without it, they'd collapse; with it, they can keep on going.

On their own power they can do absolutely nothing to make even the slightest inch of spiritual progress. For sin acts as a brake upon them, and the engines of their heart are powerless to move their spiritual lives forward with the brakes locked tight. However, by depending daily on the presence and the power of God's Spirit within them, believers can move ahead. Christ himself comes to "dwell"—literally, "to settle down in and take up residence"—ever more fully in their hearts (3:17). Receiving his regular supply of energy, believers in Jesus continue to progress toward the destination God has established for them—to become patterned and shaped more and more by Jesus himself.

Now, this source of spiritual energy is available not only to a select few, to some spiritual elite. *To every believer* who nourishes himself or herself by tapping into the power of Christ's Spirit, Jesus himself gives the promise of growth and strength.

Growing is not a quick, one-time event, of course—some brief encounter with God that brings an adrenalin burst of spiritual energy. Rather, it's a process—nothing shorter than a life-long process—of day-by-day dwelling upon and chewing the life-nourishing, power-transmitting promises and commands in God's Word. And along the way we discover that God, through his Spirit and Word, is transfusing into us fresh drops of spiritual stamina and strength—as much as we need to face our situations and overcome our circumstances.

Paul prays, too, that his readers, "being rooted and established in love, may have power, together with all the saints, to grasp how wide and long and high and deep is the love of Christ, and to know this love that surpasses knowledge" (3:17-19).

Paul's two metaphors in verse 17 are apt. He wants his readers to see that they are like flowers and leaves on a plant that continuously draws nourishment from its invisible roots. They are also placed properly ("established") on a well-laid foundation. Christ's love, the solid foundation on which Christian living is set, is also the fountain from which that living flows in "power" (3:18).

Again we see Paul return to the matter of power. This time he longs for his readers to "have power" (*exischusete*, "to be fully strong") in order to "grasp" something of the immense and vast totality of Christ's love for them (3:18). And what Paul longs for each believer to have, he desires also for all, that his friends might have this power "together with all the saints" (3:18).

Further, Paul desires that they "know this love that surpasses knowledge" (3:19). This curious phrase points to more than head knowledge, more than grasping that Christ's love is in all and through all (3:18; see 4:6). Truly *knowing* Christ's love is possible only by experience, by the sort of personal, intimate knowledge shared by close friends and, even deeper, by husbands and wives—and yet it's far deeper still. Knowing Christ is the ultimate relationship possible for us human beings. And it results, as other close relationships do, in growth and newness of life—to the utmost. As Paul says, in knowing this love we "may be filled to the measure of all the fullness of God" (3:19).

And how can we "know" the love of Christ? Through the Father's strengthening "with power through his Spirit in [our] inner being, so that Christ may dwell in [our] hearts through faith" (3:16-17). Only the efforts of the incomparably powerful Three-in-One can supply us, to the depths of our inner being, with the power "to know this love" (3:19). That's why Paul prays, for this love and the fullness it brings are only God's to give.

A Final Ascription of Praise

The size of your God governs the size of your faith. Always. Therefore, the bigger your God, the bigger your confidence in him—and also the confidence of your prayers to him. The opposite however, is not true. The size of your faith can't govern the size of your God. So never let yourself believe that anything is too big or too difficult for the one almighty God to handle. God "is able to do immeasurably more than all we ask or imagine" (3:20).

In this phrase "immeasurably more," Paul piles one superlative about God on top of another. He makes one word out of three—*hyperekperissou* literally means "over and above, quite completely, more and beyond." Paul's praying was never limited by what he with his small and finite mind thought might be possible. He knew there was an immense store of riches and power available from God, a reservoir far bigger than he could ever imagine. And, best of all, it's available to "everyone who believes" (Rom. 1:16; see Eph. 3:21).

Paul ends this exalted prayer appropriately with an ascription of glory to God "in the church," "in Christ Jesus," and "throughout all generations"—and not just in time as we know it but "for ever and ever!" (Eph. 3:21; see 1:4-6).

General Discussion

1. What do our prayers say about our "deep and sincere heart-thoughts"? What do our prayers say about the size of our God? What factors in our lives today might make it hard to "think big" in our prayer life?
2. Consider again this summary of Ephesians 3:15: "We who believe in God through faith in Jesus Christ have come to bear the very 'family likeness' of God; we reflect the traits of God's own character." Reflect together on the character of your own church. What "traits of God's own character" do you see? How do you bear the "family likeness" of God? What growth areas can you identify to bring you even closer to God's character?
3. Focusing on the requests Paul makes in Ephesians 3:16-19, comment on the statement "Paul's central desire for his readers . . . is that they may grow spiritually." In what ways do your fellow church members show their interest in growing spiritually together? In talking about their faith? In what ways might they (and you) do these things more clearly or effectively?
4. Paul prays that his readers "may have power, together with all the saints, to grasp how wide and long and high and deep is the love of Christ" (Eph. 3:18). Give one or two concrete examples of how one or more of the "saints" around you have enriched your grasp of the love of Christ. What does this say about the importance of being an active part of the fellowship of God's people?

Ideas for Small Groups

Opening (5-10 minutes)

Pray/Worship—Open with a time of prayer and worship, praising God for making it possible through Christ to approach him in prayer, and asking Christ to help each one of you grow in understanding and love as you learn about Paul's prayer for his readers. You may wish to read together

Philippians 4:4-7 and Ephesians 6:18 to help you focus on the importance of prayer and how it relates to our life together in Christ. Then take a few moments to reflect individually on times when you were built up through the prayers of fellow believers, offered either for you or for others.

Share—Share with each other, if you like, some of the examples you have been reflecting on. Now may also be a good time to share how you're doing on your goals from previous lessons and on any group projects you may have chosen.

Focus—Think about the following question and keep it in mind throughout this session: *What does my prayer life have to do with the life of the church?*

Growing (35-50 minutes)

Read (Optional)

You may want to read together the Scripture passage (as well as the study-guide notes) before moving into your discussion time.

Discuss

Before choosing from the following process questions, work through most or all of the "General Discussion" questions, which relate in various ways to prayer and fellowship and their awesome possibilities in Christ.

On prayer and fellowship in Christ:

- In what ways has this lesson challenged you to think about prayer?
- What do you enjoy about the fellowship of the church? How does this relate to your understanding of God and prayer?
- In what ways do Paul's prayer requests in this passage relate to you? To your group? To your local church?
- Share your thoughts on how you can help build up the church in Christ's power through prayer and fellowship.

Goalsetting (5 minutes)

Try working on the following goal in the coming week:

- I want to help build up the church through prayer and fellowship in the power of Christ. Here's what I'd like to pray for, and here's one way I can practice fellowship:

Closing (5-10 minutes)

Preparing for Prayer

Share items that you'd like the others in your group to bring to God in prayer for you. Mention personal concerns and praises, the goals you've set so far in this study, and so on.

Prayer

As you close your meeting with prayer, ask the Lord Jesus to live "in your hearts through faith" (Eph. 3:17) and to give you the power, together with all believers, to understand and experience his love. After everyone has joined in to offer their prayer concerns and praises, you may wish to close by reading aloud Christ's prayer in John 17:20-26, to help everyone focus on unity, the topic for the next lesson. Before parting, sing together, if you like, a song about prayer and unity such as "Lord, Listen to Your Children Praying" or "Spirit Divine, Inspire Our Prayer."

Group Project (Optional)

As a group, compose your own prayer for your church, based on what you see as its priority needs or challenges. You may want to share this prayer with your church leaders and perhaps ask if your group might offer it as part of a congregational prayer during a worship service.

7 A Plea for Christian Unity

Ephesians 4:1-10

1 As a prisoner for the Lord, then, I urge
you to live a life worthy of the calling you
have received. 2 Be completely humble and
gentle; be patient, bearing with one another
in love. 3 Make every effort to keep the unity
of the Spirit through the bond of peace.
4 There is one body and one Spirit—just as
you were called to one hope when you were
called—5 one Lord, one faith, one baptism;
6 one God and Father of all, who is over all
and through all and in all.
7 But to each one of us grace has been
given as Christ apportioned it. 8 This is why
it says:

> "When he ascended on high,
> he led captives in his train
> and gave gifts to men."

9 (What does "he ascended" mean except that
he also descended to the lower, earthly
regions? 10 He who descended is the very one
who ascended higher than all the heavens, in
order to fill the whole universe.)

The core of the biblical message is not what human beings have been able to do for God, but rather who God is and what God has done for them.

Who is God? Jewish children, even before they learned their own name, were taught to say this text: "Hear, O Israel, the LORD our God, the LORD is one" (Deut. 6:4). It states one of the most compelling and important realities about life itself. Every Jew repeated these powerful words every day for the rest of his or her life as a central confession of faith.

What has God done? God has created his people, chosen them, loved them, and rescued them. As their Father in Christ, God is now pleased to call them his children. God carries them in his arms for the rest of their days, sustains them moment by moment, and promises to bring them home. Simply put, having done no less than everything for his people, God is "over all and through all and in all." There is, therefore, "one God and Father of all" (Eph. 4:6).

From these twin central truths of who God is and what God has done, everything else in the Bible follows—including how God's people, in response, are to live.

In the first half of his letter to the Ephesian Christians Paul has set forth what the one true God has done for his people. In the second half Paul lays out for his fellow believers the implications of these core teachings for their actual life together. Who they are—God's own people—must give shape to what they do. Their identity must now bring shape to their obedience.

Note well: good doctrine—right thinking about God and his ways with his people—is vital to good ethics—right teachings about how to live. Christian doctrine that does not result in Christian ethics is sterile and incomplete; ethics without doctrine lacks solid foundation and becomes directionless and incoherent.

Live Worthily—Keep Unity

Today it often seems that we're becoming more and more polarized—in the church as well as in society. Our conversation and manners toward one another are coarsening. We're doing more shouting at one another than talking and discussing. And we're doing it with more stridency.

Within the body of Christ, believers are arming themselves with arguments, as if to get their point across. And the fault lines within the Lord's family are growing wider. Some people, it seems, would less prefer to lose an argument than a brother or sister in Christ. John Henry Newman once said, "Oh, how we hate one another for the love of Christ."

God weeps when we yell at one another. For, belonging to the "one God and Father of all" (4:6), we also belong to one another. And any form of hate—belittling and insulting by thoughts, words, looks, and gestures (see Heidelberg

Catechism Q&A 105)—is murder and thus a violation of one of God's central commands (Matt. 5:21-22).

Moved by God's Spirit, Paul pleads with his readers—and with us too—"Make every effort to keep the unity of the Spirit through the bond of peace" (Eph. 4:3).

It is from his position as a "prisoner for the Lord" (4:1) that Paul issues his appeal. He has said it before (3:1), but he must repeat it again and again. For everything, simply everything, follows from his identity in Jesus Christ. More and more, Paul is taking on the character qualities of his Lord. He can go only where Christ wants him to go, led by Christ's Spirit. Never, therefore, can Paul chart his course by the whims of public opinion. His Lord's desires are Paul's commands. And in the Spirit they are Paul's desires too.

Paul "urges" his readers (4:1). The Greek verb for "urge" (*parakaleo*) means "to summon to one's side, to call for help." To Paul, maintaining unity among believers for Christ's sake was not a take-it-or-leave-it affair—as though politeness, a cordial spirit, and an eagerness for civility are simply "nice" qualities that help us get along better together. No, to live in unity and harmony together is the Lord's command, and to do so takes effort—strong, deliberate, and daily effort. Fully aware of how difficult the task really is, Paul issues a strong summons and appeal for the sake of God's honor.

Christians are "to live a life worthy" of their calling (4:1). The word for "worthy" here (*axios*) originally meant "bringing up the other beam of the scales," "bringing into balance." In other words, the one side of their lives, *being* children of God and sharing in all the privileges of that high position, must have a corresponding counterbalance, namely, *living* as such. The "calling [they] have received" (4:1) comes from no one other than the sovereign Lord of history. Their duty to respond to it, then, is no less awesome in importance.

Features of a Worthy Life

Paul lists five specific features of a life "worthy of the calling you have received" (4:1). He begins with "Be completely humble" (4:2). The word for "humble" here (*tapeinophrosune*) means "considering or weighing with a lowly spirit." To the pagan Greek, humility was anything but a virtue. Greeks, after all, were passionate about prominence and self-importance, pride and distinction. To them, humility, the distinguishing mark among Christ's followers, was a sad, deplorable, and weak character flaw found in those who "just couldn't make it" in life. Never—not in their wildest thinking—could the Greeks imagine humility as a character quality to be pursued. Nor can many of us in today's Western society.

However strongly today we may hear the siren call to become great and make a name for ourselves, both outside the Christian fellowship and within it, we Christians must remember that in our Lord's kingdom the way down is up. And the way up, unmistakably, is down. (See Phil. 2:5-13.)

Next Paul advises his readers to be "gentle" (*praotes*—Eph. 4:2). Sometimes translated as "meek," the word does not mean "wishy-washy" or "wimpy." Rather, it means that one does not approach life and its sometimes difficult circumstances with a clenched fist and a bitter, vindictive spirit. Though they are strong, Christians are gentle in their response—controlled, not belligerent, measured, peaceable through and through.

Only those who know they belong wholly to God can be truly gentle, of course, for they are convinced that they need not take things into their own hands and clobber their opponents when things go awry and people are against them.

God's followers must also be "patient" (4:2). The Greek word here (*makrothumia*) means, literally, "steadfast, even-tempered, forbearing." Knowing that God is in control of their lives, believers need not—must not—insist on instantaneous results or a fast-paced response.

Christians are to be patient with each other—"with everyone," in fact (1 Thess. 5:14). The Greeks had little regard for this virtue also; far better, they advised, to strike back—immediately—when circumstances won't budge or people don't cooperate.

The fourth feature of a worthy Christian life is "bearing with one another in love" (Eph. 4:2). Haters increase tensions. Frustration, resentment, and anger toward another can never be stopped unless cut off from the evil air in which they thrive. The best, most potent—and most Christlike—defense against one's enemies is a strong offense: to take their evil assaults and, by bearing with these persons in selfless love (*agape*), render those assaults feeble and impotent.

Finally, Christians are "to make every effort to keep the unity of the Spirit through the bond of peace" (4:3). The original word for "make every effort" (*spoudazo*) means "to make haste, to be intent and diligent, eager." So our deliberate aim as Christians must ever be to maintain unity and peace among ourselves.

But notice that this unity is not some smooth (or rickety) strategy put together by human ingenuity and goodwill. It's the "unity of the Spirit," a gift from God to be kept and treasured by us in faith. We *are* in fact united in God through the Spirit's presence and power among us; so we are to cherish and to maintain this unity by walking in a manner worthy of our calling. Doing so, we shall be showing the world what it means to belong—together—in Christ.

Jesus' Final Plea

In his high-priestly prayer, his final prayer here on earth, Jesus pleaded with his Father, "I pray . . . that all of them may be one, Father, just as you are in me and I am in you. . . . May they be brought to complete unity to let the world know that you sent me and have loved them even as you have loved me" (John 17:20-23). Peace and unity among his followers mattered a lot to Jesus. And they matter to him still. They should, therefore, also matter to us.

But we're not left to work at these things on our own. Jesus also prayed, "Father, I want those you have given me to be with me where I am" (John 17:24), and "when he ascended," as Ephesians 4:8 puts it in the language of earthly conquerors, "he led captives in his train and gave gifts to men." This means not only that we have a place promised for us in Christ's presence for eternity (John 14:2-3), but also that we have gifts of grace we may use now to help us grow closer to God and to one another. We'll discuss several of these gifts in the next lesson, so for now we can simply reflect in awe that God empowers us through Christ and his Spirit to "make every effort to keep" our oneness in him (Eph. 4:3).

General Discussion

1. Before turning your attention to Ephesians 4, pause to reflect together on chapters 1-3. What have you learned from those chapters that motivates you to want to live a life of new obedience before the Lord?
2. How would you respond to a church member who said, "All I want are sermons that tell me how to live next week. Just tell me what I need to do and save all that doctrine stuff. I just want practical messages."
3. Look again at the first two paragraphs in the above section "Live Worthily—Keep Unity." How do you respond to the observations there? From the perspective of Ephesians 4:3-6, how would you grade your church on the issue of unity? Your denomination? The worldwide church of Christ? What barriers to unity do you see at each of these church levels?
4. On the basis of Ephesians 4:1-6, what (more) can you do to promote the unity that honors God? What (more) can your church do?
5. Why has Christ "apportioned" his gifts of grace rather than giving everyone all the gifts?

Ideas for Small Groups

Opening (5-10 minutes)

Pray/Worship—Open with prayer and a brief time of worship, praising our awesome God and celebrating what

God has done for us in Jesus Christ. Pray that each person present may experience the stirring of the Spirit to live wholly for Christ, as you focus together here on unity in the church, Christ's body. Songs you might sing during your worship time could include "Our God Is an Awesome God," "Alleluia, Sing to Jesus," and "We Are One in the Spirit."

Share—Share with each other how you're doing on your goals from previous lessons and on any group projects you may have chosen.

Focus—Consider the following question as you work through this session: *How much am I concerned about unity in the church?*

Growing (35-50 minutes)

Read (Optional)

You may want to read together the Scripture passage (along with the study-guide notes) before moving into your discussion time.

Discuss

Before choosing from the following process questions, you'll want to work through as many of the "General Discussion" questions as you have time for, especially 1, 3, and 4, which interconnect with these process questions.

On God, the church, and unity:

- Based on what you've learned in Ephesians 1-3, why do you think Paul begins his instruction on right living (chap. 4-6) with a strong emphasis on unity? What have you learned about the relationship between God, the church, and unity?
- "General Discussion" question 3 asked about barriers to unity that you've observed in the church at various levels. What barriers to unity do you see in your own life? In your small group?
- What do you know about Christ's ascension and how important it is to the worldwide church as Christ's body? (See John 16:5-15; Eph. 4:8-10.)

Goalsetting (5 minutes)

Try working on the following goal in the coming week:

- Here's how I want to apply what I've learned in this lesson about our amazing God and the unity he makes possible for us:

Closing (5-10 minutes)

Preparing for Prayer

Share items that you'd like the others in your group to bring to God in prayer for you.

Prayer

Close your meeting with prayer, asking the Lord to help each one of you persevere in living "a life worthy of the calling" of being God's children (Eph. 4:1). Ask for guidance in applying what you've learned here about unity and about God's awe-inspiring design for us as the body of Christ. Everyone may join in with their prayer concerns and praises. If you like, close with a song such as "We Are One in the Spirit," and everyone, before leaving, might wish each other the peace of the Holy Spirit in the coming week.

8 Step by Step Toward Christian Maturity

Ephesians 4:11-16

[11]It was he who gave some to be apostles, some to be prophets, some to be evangelists, and some to be pastors and teachers, [12]to prepare God's people for works of service, so that the body of Christ may be built up [13]until we all reach unity in the faith and in the knowledge of the Son of God and become mature, attaining to the whole measure of the fullness of Christ.

[14]Then we will no longer be infants, tossed back and forth by the waves, and blown here and there by every wind of teaching and by the cunning and craftiness of men in their deceitful scheming.

[15]Instead, speaking the truth in love, we will in all things grow up into him who is the Head, that is, Christ. [16]From him the whole body, joined and held together by every supporting ligament, grows and builds itself up in love, as each part does its work.

A Gift for Every Member

In 1972 Ray Stedman, a Christian pastor in Palo Alto, California, wrote in *Body Life,* "Whenever anyone, by faith in Jesus Christ, passed from the kingdom and power of Satan into the kingdom of God's love, he was immediately taught that the Holy Spirit of God had not only imparted to him the life of Jesus Christ but had also equipped him with a spiritual gift or gifts, which he was then responsible to discover and exercise." Stedman was merely echoing what the Heidelberg Catechism stated four centuries earlier: "What do you understand by 'the communion of saints'? First, that believers one and all, as members of this community, share in Christ and in all his treasures and gifts. Second, that each member should consider it a duty to use these gifts readily and cheerfully for the service and enrichment of the other members" (Q&A 55).

"He . . . gave" (Eph. 4:11)—the language here is emphatic. No person within the fellowship of Christ's community ever decides on his or her own to become or to do anything. It is Christ himself who calls and equips and who sovereignly determines how his gifts are to be distributed among the members of his body. There's no room for any triumphalist, thumbs-under-armpits attitude—or for some "excuse-me-for-breathing-I'm-not-worth-anything" attitude either. The fellowship suffers if one fails to use his or her gift—and also if others despise and demean the gift a person has been given.

No matter what they do—choir members, church school teachers, elders, deacons, sound technicians, hospitality servants, preachers—all are equipped by Christ for their task and placed by divine appointment. Roles and responsibilities within the church have nothing to do with language like "I think I'll become a . . ." Nobody ought to get it into his or her head to do anything except having heard Christ's call.

Though the list of gifts here is not exhaustive (see also Rom. 12:4-8; 1 Cor. 12:7-11, 27-30), Paul mentions five positions within the fellowship: apostles, prophets, evangelists, pastors, and teachers.

Apostles. The Greek word *apostolos* means "sent one, delegated to discharge a mission." Jesus called his original twelve apostles so "that they might be with him and that he might send them out to preach and to have authority to drive out demons" (Mark 3:14-15). In other words, they were to learn from Jesus about the kingdom of God and to herald it. Witnesses of the risen Lord, the apostles laid the foundation of the church (1 Cor. 12:28; Eph. 2:20). And once the church became established, the apostolic office came to an end.

Prophets, too, were vitally important to the founding of the church (1 Cor. 12:28; Eph. 2:20). The New Testament does not clearly delineate the task of a prophet (in a sense, each and every follower of Jesus has a prophetic office); nor does the New Testament distinguish it exactly from the office of an apostle. However, the prophet did declare the will of God with his "Thus says the Lord" (Acts 11:27-28). Like their Old

Testament counterparts, the prophets in the church clarified for the believers what God was doing in the events of history happening around them. But there were false prophets as well as true ones (1 John 4.1); therefore, the Christian fellowship always had to be alert to their messages and to discern whether they were speaking a word from the Lord.

Evangelists are mentioned only a few times in the New Testament: in Acts 21:8, in 2 Timothy 4:5, and here in Ephesians 4:11. What they did, however—to proclaim and commend the good news of Jesus—was vitally important to the early Christian fellowship. In a real sense, they were the church's first missionaries. Their vocation, "to evangelize" (*evangelizo*), is mentioned fifty-four times in the New Testament, and the "gospel" (*evangelion*) they proclaimed is mentioned seventy-six times. Lost people outside the church mattered to God—and they matter still. Evangelists are God's strategic voice in calling unbelievers to enter the fellowship of the forgiven.

Pastors and teachers (poimenas kai didaskalous). These two offices are joined together here by a common conjunction, so the two functions within the fellowship, caring for souls and teaching them, may well have been performed by one person—a shepherd-teacher, as the original Greek words imply. The responsibility of pastors and teachers was the spiritual welfare of the body of believers. As persons left the dark night of unbelief and sin and entered the light of God's hope and joy, it was the pastors' and teachers' job to build these persons up and help them mature spiritually.

Since the Bible here and elsewhere strongly emphasizes that all believers have gifts, every Christian ought to discern his or her gift(s) deliberately and carefully. Gifts used in honor of Christ and in service to one another are strategically important to the welfare of Christ's body.

But how do you discern your gift? It takes listening. Listening to God's Word as it teaches about gifts. Listening to yourself as you try honestly to assess what your abilities and passions are. Listening to the counsel and advice of wise people, others who know you well. And, finally, listening to God through prayer as he calls you to your task.

Toward Spiritual Maturity

God has a specific purpose in giving us gifts: "so that the body of Christ may be built up until we all reach unity in the faith and . . . become mature, attaining to the whole measure of the fullness of Christ" (Eph. 4:12-13). Without gifts, believers would remain "infants, tossed back and forth by the waves, and blown here and there by every wind of teaching" (4:14).

The deepest and most ardent longing God has for the church—the very reason for its existence—is to help believers become all they're meant to be in Jesus—to attain "the fullness of Christ" (4:13). A believer who eventually dies and departs the earthly body of Christ ought to look a lot more like Jesus than the day he or she entered it. Never, therefore, can the church remain static. It ought *always* to be changing—growing toward what God intends. Growing Christians are always alert to the dangerous attitude that lurks behind what Martin Marty calls the "Seven Last Words of the Church": "We've never done it this way before." A "let's never change" attitude fossilizes a church and stifles an eagerness to grow.

All other purposes for God's church—evangelism, relief of the world's social distress, moral influence upon a wicked society, providing safe haven from the world's evil, and so on—flow out of God's foundational purpose to grow "all" believers into spiritually mature daughters and sons (4:13).

Unity, Truth, Love

Paul does not talk about "maturity in general"; he lists specific benchmarks: growth in unity, in truth, and in love.

Christians must become more and more unified. In 4:2 Paul has encouraged his readers to keep unity in the Spirit and to be bound together in peace (lesson 7). Here he calls for two additional dimensions of that unity. We must reach "unity in the faith and in the knowledge of the Son of God" (4:13). More and more, God's people must come to know—with their heads and in their hearts—the unsearchable depths of God's love for them expressed in Christ (Rom. 11:33-36) and of the power of Christ's resurrection within them (Phil. 3:10). Together believers must study God's truth more and more; together they must come to trust him more and more. Doing both, they will inevitably grow in the unity God intends.

As Christians learn to "[speak] the truth" (Eph. 4:15), they will grow into spiritual adulthood. No longer will they be like infants, ignorant, vacillating, interested one moment in one thing and the next moment in another. Rather, they will have stability and rootedness (3:17). They will not fall prey to every whim and fad that comes along. In an age as relativistic and rootless as ours, Christians must learn the importance of being nourished daily by truth, the truth that is "in Christ Jesus." Together they will choose to stay close to God's Word. They will chew upon its truths, for these truths alone can bring them life and stability in a dead and rootless society.

Finally, unity and truth must be permeated by love within the Christian fellowship. Without love, unity and truth are sterile. What good is it, lacking love, to be unified in grim duty? What good is it, lacking love, to be impeccably—and acridly—orthodox? Further, telling the truth without love can be divisive, bringing disunity. Love freshens the body of Christ, keeps the unity among its members vibrant and bright, and produces a truth-telling that is fragrant, full, and wonderfully nourishing. (See 1 Cor. 13.)

In Sum

Spiritual growth is not a momentary event. It's a lifelong process. As the catechism indicates, "Even the holiest have only a small beginning of [perfect] obedience. Nevertheless . . . they do begin to live according to all, not only some, of God's commandments" (Q&A 114).

Nor can one grow optimally in isolation. Depending together upon God, we also need one another's help. Thus Paul speaks of "the whole body, joined and held together by every supporting ligament, grow[ing] and build[ing] itself up in love, as each part does its work" (Eph. 4:16).

Oh, for the body of Christ to function as God intends! If it did, people would throng en masse to come on board. It would be so attractive to wandering and lost people that they would discover, perhaps for the first time, what life is really all about. And they'd absolutely love it.

General Discussion

1. What does Christ's giving of various gifts have to do with unity?
2. Notice that in Ephesians 4:11 the gifts given by Christ are not particular functions, as described in Romans 12:3-8 and 1 Corinthians 12. The gifts are particular people! What's the significance of this unique perspective in Ephesians 4? Why does Paul mention these gifts (people) here? According to God's design, what special role do they play in the church?
3. In the comments on Ephesians 4:12-13 we read that "the deepest and most ardent longing God has for the church . . . is to help believers become all they're meant to be in Jesus—to attain 'the fullness of Christ.'" Is this longing for spiritual maturity a priority in your church? How do you know?
4. "One of the greatest attractions to Christianity is the church. Many people are attracted to community even before they are attracted to Christ!" In the light of Ephesians 4:15-16, how do you respond to this statement?
5. In Ephesians 4:15 Paul mentions "speaking the truth in love." What happens in the church when we are long on truth and short on love? How about when the opposite happens? Do you see evidence of either extreme in the church today? Why is it important to maintain both truth and love?

Ideas for Small Groups

Opening (5-10 minutes)

Pray—Open your meeting with prayer to the God who is the giver of "every good and perfect gift" (James 1:17), asking for insight and direction as you learn more about gifts and unity and how they relate to maturity in Christ.

Share—Share with each other how you're doing on your goals from previous lessons, and take this time to report on any group projects you may have decided to do.

Focus—As you work through this session, focus on the following question: *What do I know about spiritual maturity?*

Growing (35-50 minutes)

Read (Optional)

You may want to read together the Scripture passage for this lesson (as well as the study-guide notes) before moving into your discussion time.

Discuss

Before choosing from the following process questions, you'll want to work through most or all of the "General Discussion" questions, especially 1, 2, 3, and 5, which touch on spiritual gifts, unity, and maturity.

On gifts, unity, and maturity in Christ:

- Give an example or two of how Christ's gift of a leader in ministry helped to build up your church. In what ways did this build you up personally?
- What do you expect of your minister(s)? How do your expectations compare with the teaching of Ephesians 4:11-13? List one or two things you can do to help support your minister(s) and other church leaders.
- How would you "speak the truth in love" to a church member who said, "I get so upset about people who call themselves Christians but don't do a thing for the church. On any Sunday I can look down my pew and see that most of the people sitting there aren't half as mature as I am."

Goalsetting (5 minutes)

Try working on the following goal in the coming week:

- Here's how I want to apply what I've learned about the relation between gifts, unity, and maturity in this lesson:

Closing (5-10 minutes)

Preparing for Prayer

Share items that you'd like the others in your group to bring to God in prayer for you.

Prayer

End your meeting with prayer, asking the Lord to help you remember, in all that you do, that gifts, unity, and maturity in Christ are so closely related that they can't be pried apart without damaging the body of Christ and God's mission in this world. Group members may join in with their prayer concerns and praises. Then close by asking Christ to help each one of you appreciate the people he has given you to minister in the Word so that the church may continue to be built up for his sake.

Group Project/Study Goal (Optional)

Some or all of your group members may wish to learn more about their spiritual gifts and how to use them in living for Christ as part of his church today. Your pastor or education leader may be able to schedule a workshop that some or all of you could attend. Several excellent studies on spiritual gifts are available, including the newly revised *Discover Your Gifts* workshop by CRC Publications. Call 1-800-333-8300 (US) or 1-800-263-4252 (CAN) for more information.

9 Children of Darkness, Children of Light

Ephesians 4:17-32

17 So I tell you this, and insist on it in the
Lord, that you must no longer live as the
Gentiles do, in the futility of their thinking.
18 They are darkened in their understanding
and separated from the life of God because
of the ignorance that is in them due to the
hardening of their hearts. 19 Having lost all
sensitivity, they have given themselves over
to sensuality so as to indulge in every kind of
impurity, with a continual lust for more.
20 You, however, did not come to know
Christ that way. 21 Surely you heard of him
and were taught in him in accordance with
the truth that is in Jesus. 22 You were taught,
with regard to your former way of life, to
put off your old self, which is being
corrupted by its deceitful desires; 23 to be
made new in the attitude of your minds;
24 and to put on the new self, created to be
like God in true righteousness and holiness.
25 Therefore each of you must put off
falsehood and speak truthfully to his
neighbor, for we are all members of one
body. 26 "In your anger do not sin": Do not
let the sun go down while you are still angry,
27 and do not give the devil a foothold. 28 He
who has been stealing must steal no longer,
but must work, doing something useful with
his own hands, that he may have something
to share with those in need.
29 Do not let any unwholesome talk come
out of your mouths, but only what is helpful
for building others up according to their
needs, that it may benefit those who listen.
30 And do not grieve the Holy Spirit of God,
with whom you were sealed for the day of
redemption. 31 Get rid of all bitterness, rage
and anger, brawling and slander, along with
every form of malice. 32 Be kind and
compassionate to one another, forgiving
each other, just as in Christ God forgave
you.

Though we Christians do live in the world, spiritually we are set apart from it (see John 17:14-18). For there's a huge chasm—what our Reformed ancestors called the "antithesis"—between believers and unbelievers. God himself has introduced this division by calling his church into existence from out of the world. Nothing, therefore, can ever bridge the spiritual gap that exists between the church and the world, between the "children of darkness" and the "children of light" (Eph. 5:8).

The church must continually preserve its spiritual distinctiveness and clear identity in the midst of the evil of this world. After all, how can it ever call the world to repentance from its tired and sin-sick ways if the church conforms to the world?

Each and every Christian, too, must listen to the call to be "genuinely sorry for sin, to hate it more and more, and to run away from it" (Heidelberg Catechism Q&A 89), delighting only in doing the things that delight the heart of God. The process is called conversion, and it's a daily—hourly, even minute-by-minute—activity.

"No Longer!"

In Ephesians 4:17-32 Paul calls the Ephesian Christians to leave their former way of life and to live as the people they have now become in the power of Christ. The apostle begins his appeal with "So" (literally, "Therefore"). In view of all that God has done for them (Eph. 4:11-16), Paul "insist[s] on it in the Lord" that believers must now "no longer live as the Gentiles do" (4:17). For these Gentiles are groping about in darkness. They are far, far away from the life available in God (*apellotriomenoi* means "having been alienated," "enemy-like"). Unbelief and evil are never neutral: they are aggressively pitted against God and resistant to new life in the Lord.

Why this opposition of unbelievers? It issues from "the ignorance that is in them due to the hardening of their hearts" (4:18). Sometimes ignorance is bliss; often it is innocent. In the case of these unbelievers, however, ignorance proceeds from perverse hard-heartedness. These people could have—should have—known better than to act in unbelief as they do. For God has revealed himself to everyone (Rom. 1:18-25). So in callous disregard they have determined to squelch what they know and to disobey God. In the Bible "hardness of heart" means an attitude of persistent and blatant disregard of God and his ways. What these unbelievers have continued to do for so long, namely, to resist God's desires, now renders them permanently incapable of doing anything else. Their hearts are stone-hard, "having lost all sensitivity" (Eph. 4:19).

The New Self in Christ

"You, however . . ."—Paul emphatically contrasts the new life of one who is now in Christ with the "former way of life" (4:22). Not only have believers "heard" of Christ and taken their lessons in his school (4:21; literally, "learned from him"); what's more, they have "put off" the old self (4:22; see Rom. 6:6; Col. 3:9) and "put on the new self" (Eph. 4:24). This is the metaphor for the process of daily conversion. They have left behind a pattern of living that was "corrupted"—ruined, rotten, despoiled—by perverse desires (4:22). And they have put on a life fresh and bright, thoroughly renewed.

Renewal is a total and pervasive cutting out of the rotten core, a surgery so deep that one becomes a new person in the process. The overhaul begins with a decisive first step—the verbs for "put off" and "put on" indicate deliberate action—and the process continues with daily taking that step again and again. "To be made new in the attitude of [our] minds" (4:23) reveals how we can put off the old and put on the new—our way of thinking, our mind, gets a thorough scrubbing from God. The result is a person who has returned to the way he or she is supposed to be: "created to be like God in true righteousness and holiness" (4:24).

Putting the New Life into Practice

Paul now gets very specific in prescribing patterns of life that will contribute to believers' putting off the old self and putting on the new. His first appeal is this: "You must put off falsehood and speak truthfully" (4:25). Both in the Old Testament and in the New (see Ex. 20:16; Ps. 12; Matt. 5:33-37; 2 Cor. 2:17), God continually warns against pretense and artificiality. God hates any hint of deceitful duality, of saying one thing while meaning another, of acting one way while thinking another, of covering up how one really thinks and feels by plastic posturing. Lying, of whatever sort, is a pattern of activity that indicates one is not living by the fresh principles of Christ. For our Lord calls for authenticity. Among the fellowship of God's people, then, truthfulness ought to hold sway. For "we are all members of one body" (Eph. 4:25).

Second, believers are to deal with their anger (4:26-27). The anger Paul mentions here (*parorgismos*) is no momentary hot-headedness, a brief spilling over of turbulent emotions. Rather, it's a focused, relentless, determined, driven anger, powered by the deep energy of hate that can drive a person day after day, feed upon one's spirit, and eventually consume him or her. Such anger is vindictive. The only countermeasure to its terrible power is to deal with it quickly and regularly—every day before nightfall, in fact, so its ugliness won't carry over into the next day.

Third, stealing must surrender to sharing (4:28). Before their conversion, these early Christians participated in all kinds of low-life practices, including cheating and swindling others; sometimes they violently robbed. "Whatever the method, it's got to stop," says Paul. "Replace your evil practice by doing 'something good'—something honest and generous—with your hands. Work for what you get, so that you may share with those in need." (For an amazingly current application of Paul's command here, see Heidelberg Catechism Q&A 110-111.) Paul himself lived by his own advice here. Wherever he went on his missionary journeys, he worked for his food so as not to have to leech from anyone (1 Thess. 2:9; 2 Thess. 3:6-15).

Fourth, Paul counsels his Ephesian friends to stop their gush of "rotten words" (*sapros* means "foul, unwholesome, spoiled"). This is the only time this vivid adjective is used in the New Testament to describe something other than decomposed fruit, vegetables, fish, trees, and so on. Christians need to rid their vocabulary of what we call "coarse words," "foul speech," "gutter language"—and yet Paul means much more. Some words, however good in themselves, can be spoken at the wrong time or expressed in the wrong way so as to wound and even kill a person. Hence the clear warning of Heidelberg Catechism Q&A 105: "I am not to belittle, insult, hate, or kill my neighbor—not by my thoughts, my words, my look or gesture. . . ." (See also Rom. 12:17-21.)

Once again, Paul advises replacing an evil practice with a good one: speak "only what is helpful for building others up according to their needs, that it may benefit those who listen" (Eph. 4:29). Graciousness ought to mark the speech of every person maturing in Christ. As Proverbs 25:11 says, "A word aptly spoken is like apples of gold in settings of silver."

Fifth, Paul warns his readers to "get rid of bitterness, rage and anger, brawling and slander, along with every form of malice" (4:31)—a motley mass of ugliness proceeding from a mean and vengeful spirit. God's people must become "kind and compassionate to one another, forgiving each other." To do so is only right and fitting, for that's how God has treated them: "in Christ God forgave you" (4:32).

An Invitation to Careful Inspection

Paul's teaching in this section of his letter invites us to take a solemn and honest look at who we are and how we live, and then, depending upon God, to resolve again to live as the Lord commands. It is prudent, then, to

- know how powerful evil really is, and how weak we are in our efforts to resist it.
- understand that not every area of temptation is equally alluring. We are wise to be honest and clear about the areas where we're especially vulnerable.
- understand how temptation works: seeing leads to imagining, imagining to doing, doing to habits, and habits to character (see Matt. 18:8-9). We must stop temptation where it starts, staying away from areas where we're especially weak.
- develop a spiritual companionship—an accountability relationship—with at least one other person. That person can become a messenger ("angel") of God, helping us to resist evil.
- Pray regularly for the Spirit's presence and power.

In his *Imitation of Christ*, Thomas à Kempis said, "Every day we ought to renew our purpose and refresh ourselves as though it were the first day of our conversion."

General Discussion

1. "The church must continually preserve its spiritual distinctiveness and clear identity in the midst of the evil of this world." In your estimation, how is the church in North America doing in the area of preserving its "spiritual distinctiveness"?
2. In practical terms, what does it mean to you to put off the old self and put on the new? What makes the daily process of "putting off" and "putting on" difficult?
3. Paul begins his appeal for a distinctive Christian lifestyle with that significant word "So" (meaning "therefore"—Eph. 4:17). What does this word refer to? What motivation did Paul have in mind to move his readers to leave behind (and keep behind them) their former way of life?
4. In Ephesians 4:25-32 Paul specifies five practical ways for his readers to put off the old and put on the new. Review these together and comment on the relevance of each one for Christian living today.
5. Review together the five points of advice at the end of the author's comments above. How do you react to each of these? What items, if any, would you add in resolving to apply Ephesians 4:17-32 to your daily living?

Ideas for Small Groups

Opening (5-10 minutes)

Pray—Open with prayer, asking God to help each one of you focus on the important advice in today's Scripture passage for our daily living in Christ.

Share—Share with each other how you're doing on your goals from previous lessons, and take this time to report on any group projects you may have decided to do. *Note:* This lesson about leaving the old life of sin and living for Jesus will fit in well with a brief discussion of the book *Not the Way It's Supposed to Be,* if any of you have opted to do the "Group Study Project" mentioned in lesson 3.

Focus—As you work through this session, try to keep this focus question in mind: *In what ways does my living for Christ set me apart in this world?*

Growing (35-50 minutes)

Read (Optional)

You may want to read together the Scripture passage for this lesson (along with the study-guide notes) before moving into your discussion time.

Discuss

Before choosing from the following process questions, try working through the "General Discussion" questions, all of which relate well to small group study on living distinctively for Christ.

On distinctive living for Christ:

- What have you learned (or relearned) in this lesson about living for Christ? Has anything surprised you? Surprised you about yourself? Explain.
- In connection with "General Discussion" question 3, what motivates you to put off the old way of life and to keep it behind you?
- In connection with "General Discussion" question 5, what do you know about temptation and how dangerous it is? Share, if you like, how you avoid certain temptations that are hard for you to resist.
- Describe, if you wish, one or two experiences in which prayer for the Spirit's power has helped you in your living for Christ.

Goalsetting (5 minutes)

Try working on one of the following goals in the coming week:

- I want to dedicate (or rededicate) myself to living distinctively for Christ. I need to work on these areas of my life, in the Spirit's power:
- Here's how I want to apply what I've learned in this lesson about living for Christ:

Closing (5-10 minutes)

Preparing for Prayer

Share items that you'd like the others in your group to bring to God in prayer for you.

Prayer

Close with prayer, thanking God for providing a way for us to put off our old selves and put on our new selves in Christ. Ask the Holy Spirit to help each one of you see any "old ways" in your living that need to be cast off, and pray for strength and direction in putting on new ways of living for Christ. Everyone may join in with prayer concerns and praises. Before parting till your next meeting, you may wish to sing together the familiar hymn "Living for Jesus" or another song about giving our lives over completely to Christ.

10 Above Reproach, Indisputably

Ephesians 5:1-21

[1]Be imitators of God, therefore, as dearly loved children [2]and live a life of love, just as Christ loved us and gave himself up for us as a fragrant offering and sacrifice to God. [3]But among you there must not be even a hint of sexual immorality, or of any kind of impurity, or of greed, because these are improper for God's holy people. [4]Nor should there be obscenity, foolish talk or coarse joking, which are out of place, but rather thanksgiving. [5]For of this you can be sure: No immoral, impure or greedy person—such a man is an idolater—has any inheritance in the kingdom of Christ and of God. [6]Let no one deceive you with empty words, for because of such things God's wrath comes on those who are disobedient. [7]Therefore do not be partners with them.

[8]For you were once darkness, but now you are light in the Lord. Live as children of light [9](for the fruit of the light consists in all goodness, righteousness and truth) [10]and find out what pleases the Lord. [11]Have nothing to do with the fruitless deeds of darkness, but rather expose them. [12]For it is shameful even to mention what the disobedient do in secret. [13]But everything exposed by the light becomes visible, [14]for it is light that makes everything visible. This is why it is said:

"Wake up, O sleeper,
 rise from the dead,
and Christ will shine on you."

[15]Be very careful, then, how you live—not as unwise but as wise, [16]making the most of every opportunity, because the days are evil. [17]Therefore do not be foolish, but understand what the Lord's will is. [18]Do not get drunk on wine, which leads to debauchery. Instead, be filled with the Spirit. [19]Speak to one another with psalms, hymns and spiritual songs. Sing and make music in your heart to the Lord, [20]always giving thanks to God the Father for everything, in the name of our Lord Jesus Christ.

[21]Submit to one another out of reverence for Christ.

"Be what you is, 'cause if you is what you ain't, then you ain't what you is." These words from an old Southern preacher fittingly summarize what Paul is teaching his readers in Ephesians 5. The apostle is calling us as followers of Christ to live with integrity.

Nowadays we need all the reminders and encouragements to integrity that we can get. Good models of it are hard to come by, while poor models abound. Ivan Boesky, Pete Rose, Ben Jonson, Jim Bakker, Jimmy Swaggart, Richard Nixon—the very names of these leaders bring up images of deceit. Their lives, in part, have reflected pretense, artificiality, sham, and posturing. There's a distance between what they've said and what they've done.

The only difference between these persons and the rest of us, though, is that they were caught—glaringly—and we, perhaps, have not been. But each of us, if we're honest, must admit that continually we struggle with the issue of "being real."

In his book *Authentic Christianity* Ray Stedman suggests there are three ways in which we Christians handle slippage in our Christian walk. Some—a small minority—are honest enough to admit their missteps; they repent, beg forgiveness from God and others, and try to walk in integrity again. Others simply keep on doing what they've been doing: walking away from Jesus Christ, who calls them to follow him, and eventually they lose their way totally. A third group, however, discovers another way to handle wrongdoing. They persist in doing wrong while at the same time avoiding the public embarrassment and shame that confession brings. It's a game called "Let's pretend." They act as though they're living a holy life when they're not.

Integrity means wholeness, single-mindedness, confident and right living. It means knowing the difference between right and wrong—and then being willing to act upon that knowledge, no matter what the circumstances.

Who We Are

Paul begins his clarion call to live with integrity by reminding his readers who they are: God's "dearly loved children" (Eph. 5:1). Believers are neither orphans nor outcasts; they are part of the divine family. God, through Christ, has become their heavenly Father. And in much the same way that earthly children imitate their parents, these heavenly sons and daughters—and we—are to imitate God (5:1). Jesus challenged his disciples to do the same as he spoke about loving their enemies: "Be perfect . . . as your heavenly Father is perfect" (Matt. 5:48).

In connection with this we are called to "live a life of love" (Eph. 5:2). The actual verb Paul uses is "to walk in love," a favorite metaphor for advancing and making progress in the Christian way. Of course, there are lots of ways in which we, simply because we are human (and sinfully so), cannot imitate God himself. But we *can* love, even as God does.

There is no greater evidence of this divine love for us than that "Christ loved us and gave himself up for us as a fragrant offering and sacrifice to God" (5:2). In view of what Christ has done, says Paul, only one response from us is utterly right and fitting: day by day our conduct must become more consistent with who we are. Some actions are right; others are wrong—clearly so. The verses that follow (5:3-14) set forth the deep contrasts between what it means to be "children of light" and "children of darkness" (5:8), between those who are awake and those who are asleep (5:14), between those who are "foolish" and those who are "wise" (5:15, 17). In effect, these verses summarize what it means to put off the "old self" and put on the new, as Paul teaches in 4:22-32.

Not Even a Hint

Paul's warning is bracing and direct: "Among you there must not be even a hint of sexual immorality, or of any kind of impurity, or of greed, because these are improper for God's holy people" (5:3). The original word for "sexual immorality" here is *porneia*, meaning "fornication." What a mighty revolution the first Christians introduced into the prevailing sexual ethic of their day. While among the Greeks it was considered inappropriate for women to have sexual relations with anyone but their husbands, men were allowed extramarital relations. Christianity, however, put both men and women on an equal footing in this regard. Godlike purity demanded that no one was to have sexual relations with anyone but his or her spouse.

But not just the act of adultery was to be avoided; even "any kind of impurity" (*akatharsia pasa*) was to be avoided. This referred to the very behaviors that can incite unchastity and actual adultery, such as "actions, looks, talk, thoughts, or desires" (Heidelberg Catechism Q&A 109)—a prudent warning for a society (like ours) that was massively sated with every imaginable kind of sexual expression, however kinky and kooky.

Spiritual director that he is, Paul shakes a stiff finger of caution toward any who might be tempted toward "obscenity, foolish talk or coarse joking" (Eph. 5:4). Paul's word here for "coarse joking" (*eutrapelia*) does not refer to lighthearted, bright speech, good humor, convivial and warm banter. It refers to base, perverted jesting—filthy talk. God's people ought never to participate in such depraved activity, no matter where they are or what they're doing—even if they're "just out with the boys" or if it's "girls' night out."

Perverse talk, no matter what circumstances it takes place in, is never harmless or excusable. It hurts—always. Actions have consequences. Though Joe or Jessie Average suppose that both their public and secret perversions do not raise God's blood pressure and evoke his anger, they are foolishly—

tragically—wrong. Evildoers invite "God's wrath" (*orge*—5:6). One can take sin too seriously, supposing that wrongdoing can never be forgiven. One can also take it not seriously enough, belittling the fact that sin is an awesome and grievous affront to a holy and just God.

God, claims the Heidelberg Catechism (Q&A 10), is "terribly angry about the sin we are born with as well as the sins we personally commit." For in the depths of his being God *hates* evil. And he will deal justly with "those who are disobedient" (Eph. 5:6). Never too often can this solemn warning be repeated in our society today, which assumes that God, like a doddering grandfather on the sidelines of life, dozes off in unconcern while people sin. "The days"—this present age and society—"are evil" (5:16)—unspeakably so.

Living Fully and Well

Having warned his Ephesian friends what they are to avoid, Paul also tells them what they are to embrace. "Thanksgiving" must replace obscenity, foolish talk, and coarse joking (5:4). Life itself is a gift. To use it properly, then, means we are to celebrate and enjoy the gift itself—to revel in it, like an awestruck child at Christmas—and then to bless the Giver (5:20). We might even whistle or sing a song now and then, making "music in our hearts to the Lord" (5:19).

A wag once commented that most people live until they are thirty and die when they are seventy. Far better, as Paul says, to make "the most of every opportunity" (5:16). Live like the old Puritan whose epitaph says it all: "He lived until he died." Longing to know God in every situation and striving to do his will during every moment the Lord provides—this is what Paul means by "making the most of every opportunity" (literally, "redeeming the time"—5:16). We are to live fully and well, no matter how short or long our lives are.

But how can we not only determine to be "wise" (5:15) but also carry it out in practice? For our minds are so weak and tired; even worse, our wills are weaker still. By ourselves we simply *cannot* do what we know we should (Rom. 7:14-25).

Two things are important. First, we must rely daily upon God, declaring again and again our dependence on him "for everything" (Eph. 5:20). For we really need his presence and extraordinary power; we need to "be filled with the Spirit" (5:18). Thus, says Paul, everything we do must be done "in the name of our Lord Jesus Christ" (5:20).

Second, a fellow-battler can help—immensely. She or he can serve as a spiritual accountability partner, someone who is on our side in our furious struggle with evil. About these relationships of mutual accountability Paul says, "Submit to one another out of reverence for Christ" (5:21). Such partners can pray for each other, help each other to remain honest and authentic, and spot areas in each other's lives where they are especially vulnerable. We really do need one another in our battle against evil.

Deceit is rampant in our society. Everywhere we look, especially within our own hearts, we find it turning persons into impostors and societies into massive displays of trickery and subterfuge.

But Christians can be—must be—refreshingly different. Contrasting the ancient Israelites, who tried to live by the small supply of their own tired spiritual energy, with those who now live by the energy that Christ supplies, Paul says, "We, who with unveiled faces all reflect the Lord's glory, are being transformed into his likeness with ever-increasing glory, which comes from the Lord, who is the Spirit" (2 Cor. 3:18). Depending on our Lord and being continually renewed by his Spirit, Christians can be above reproach, indisputably.

General Discussion

1. In the light of Ephesians 5:1-2, how would you respond to this opinion: "If we really want the world to see that we are God's family, we have to be more bold to stand up for what is right. We have to stop pussyfooting around with sin and start telling it like it is!"

2. What evidence do you see in North American society, and in your own life, that the warnings in Ephesians 5:3-4 are hardly making a dent in our lives today? Why does Paul add that these evils should be replaced with thankfulness?
3. The apostle urges us to "have nothing to do with the fruitless deeds of darkness" (Eph. 5:11). How can we apply this command in our own lives? How is it that we "children of light" can "expose" such fruitless deeds?
4. What does it mean to "be filled with the Spirit"? (Eph. 5:18).
5. In his commentary on Ephesians, Andrew Lincoln states, "The drawing of specific boundaries between the Church and the world is a task that each generation of Christians has to perform for its own time and place." How do you think the church in North America is doing today in drawing those boundaries? How can we improve in our effort to be more "authentic" as "children of light"?

Ideas for Small Groups

Opening (5-10 minutes)

Pray—Open your session with prayer, asking the Lord to help you learn and grow as you study more about living a life pleasing to God in the example of Christ, who "loved us and gave himself up for us" (5:2).

Share—Share how you're doing on your goals from previous lessons, and report on any group projects you may have decided to do.

Focus—As you work through this session, try to keep this focus question in mind: *What does it mean for me to imitate God?*

Growing (35-50 minutes)

Read (Optional)

Before moving into your discussion time, you may wish to read together the Scripture for this lesson and the comments in the study guide.

Discuss

Before choosing from the following process questions, try working through some or all of the "General Discussion" questions.

On walking daily in love:

- What have you learned about imitating God in this lesson? About thankfulness? About being filled with the Spirit?
- In the light of the Scripture for this lesson, in what ways can you improve in your daily walk with God?
- In your living for Christ, give one or two examples of how you try to be "in the world but not of the world." When you've slipped up and have had to try again, what lessons have you learned?

Goalsetting (5 minutes)

Try working on the following goal in the coming week:

- I want to improve in the following ways in my daily walk of trying to imitate God:

Closing (5-10 minutes)

Preparing for Prayer

Share items that you'd like the others in your group to bring to God in prayer for you.

Prayer

Close your meeting with prayer, asking God to give each one of you a special measure of grace as you try to "live a life of love" for Jesus' sake (5:2). Everyone may join in with prayer concerns and praises. Encourage each other to "be filled with the Spirit" and, before parting, choose a favorite song or two with which you can "speak to one another" and "make music in your heart[s] to the Lord" (5:19).

11 Husbands and Wives in Christ

Ephesians 5:21-33

21Submit to one another out of reverence
for Christ.
22Wives, submit to your husbands as to
the Lord. 23For the husband is the head of
the wife as Christ is the head of the church,
his body, of which he is the Savior. 24Now as
the church submits to Christ, so also wives
should submit to their husbands in
everything.
25Husbands, love your wives, just as
Christ loved the church and gave himself up
for her 26to make her holy, cleansing her by
the washing with water through the word,
27and to present her to himself as a radiant
church, without stain or wrinkle or any
other blemish, but holy and blameless. 28In
this same way, husbands ought to love their
wives as their own bodies. He who loves his
wife loves himself. 29After all, no one ever
hated his own body, but he feeds and cares
for it, just as Christ does the church—30for
we are members of his body. 31"For this
reason a man will leave his father and
mother and be united to his wife, and the
two will become one flesh." 32This is a
profound mystery—but I am talking about
Christ and the church. 33However, each one
of you also must love his wife as he loves
himself, and the wife must respect her
husband.

Transformed Relationships

In Ephesians 5:21 Paul sets forth the fundamental pattern that ought to prevail among Christians: "Submit to one another out of reverence for Christ." John Calvin refers to this as "a mutual servitude" coupled with love for one another. In the following several verses Paul applies this important paradigm to three specific kinds of relationships: between husbands and wives (Eph. 5:22-33), between parents and children (6:1-4), and between masters and slaves (6:5-9). In each of these sorts of relationships, care and concern for the other must take precedence over one's own interests and welfare. Duties toward the other, in line with God's will, are what's important.

In this lesson and in the next we'll discuss these relationships and how they are *transformed in Christ.* We begin here with Paul's teachings on marriage.

Christian Marriage

The longer I study this exalted passage on marriage, the more these adjectives press upon my mind: *grateful, ignorant, challenged, shamed, awestruck.* Like ticks, these five words burrow in deeper and deeper. I hear God himself speaking unmistakably to me, beckoning me—again—to undertake the steep and grand climb toward what he intends Christian marriage to be.

Grateful

Two thousand years of history have dulled the revolutionary nature of what Paul wrote here about marriage. We now take so much of his teaching for granted. Back then, however, both Greeks and Jews considered women inferior. Wives had few, if any, rights. Men were allowed to divorce their wives on a whim—with a simple "bill of divorcement." Worse still, God-fearing Jews daily intoned this prayer: "Lord, I thank you that you have made me neither Gentile, nor dog, nor woman." It was a man's world back then—sadly, sinfully, indisputably.

But then the liberating good news of Jesus began to sound forth. Speaking on behalf of Christ, who died to free them and who rose from death to empower both wives and husbands to become all they're meant to be, Paul commands, "Husbands, love your wives, just as Christ loved the church . . ." (5:25).

So I'm grateful. I'm grateful to God for creating marriage in the first place (Gen. 2:18-25)—and for cleaning up spousal relationships and putting them on track again in Christ after they had become so dirty and bent by struggles over power, prestige, and worth. I'm grateful, too, for God's gracing my life with some splendid models of how marriage, at its best, can be.

Marriage is among the most remarkable gifts God has given humankind. Restored in Christ, it's a sheer wonder of grace. In some ways our modern world is still a man's world, like that ancient one that became so tired and worn out through holding women down in its vise-grip of oppression. So in the Spirit's power we all have to keep working to break down the alienation that our sin brings between man and woman.

Ignorant

There are parts of Paul's teaching about marriage that are not fully clear to me. I am so limited in my understanding and ignorant about what God intends here.

Paul commands, "Wives, submit to your husbands as to the Lord" (Eph. 5:22). I'll freely admit that I'm not sure exactly how this injunction is to be obeyed nowadays. The command here is not in the imperative voice in the original Greek text. Rather, it's a participle (*hypotassomenoi)* and is part of a series of participles that begins in 5:19: literally translated, these participles are "speaking . . . singing . . . psalming . . . giving thanks . . . being subject to [or, submitting]." Each of these, of course, is a godly thing to do and is a mark of a Spirit-filled, Christlike attitude and life. Each and every one of us who is in Christ, whether we're male or female, ought to be doing all of these all of the time.

Within marriage, Paul is saying, wives ought to be practicing the godly virtue of submitting themselves to their husbands—and doing so, no less, "as to the Lord" himself. Now, husbands ought never to take this to mean that they may "boss" their wives around. "Bossism" of whatever sort—mental, emotional, or physical tyranny—is never, never allowed in the husbandly role. But after I've finished ditching this command round with every proper proviso and precaution, and after I'm done spelling out what it doesn't allow husbands to be and to do toward their wives, I'm still left with this complex, niggling question: How are husbands and wives to arrange their day-to-day interactions with each other so that God's command to wives to submit is obeyed and yet the God-given equality of both husband and wife in Christ is not violated in the process?

H. L. Mencken once commented that for every profoundly complex matter, if one searches long and hard enough, a simple answer is usually available. But, he added, it is also usually wrong. Mencken's dictum applies to me here. For in this matter, as in most of my life's matters, I've discovered that to come up with decent principles and theories is not too difficult, but to work them out and carry them through in practice is an entirely different matter.

Challenged

Few words in Scripture touch me more deeply or compellingly than these from Paul: "Husbands, love your wives, just as Christ loved the church . . ." (5:25). They're a bracing and uncompromising command to me—no ifs, ands, or buts about it. The command challenges me to my very core.

Paul summons up the heady Greek word *agapao* here, and puts it in the imperative (*agapesate*). It's among his favorite words to describe how we ought to act like Christ, who, though innocent of all wrongdoing, unselfishly loved his people so much that he chose the way of the cross for us.

Paul fires off five verbs to indicate the depth and breadth of Christ's love and to highlight what our Lord did for us, his church. Christ "loved" his church, "gave himself up for her" (5:25), longs "to make her holy"; and is "cleansing her" (5:26). And eventually, having completed his loving, serving work on her behalf, he will "present her" (5:27) as his wonderfully pure and fully radiant bride. What a life of self-sacrificing love our Lord has shown to us!

And what a lofty pattern he has provided me to follow! The early church father John Chrysostom said,

[Husbands] . . . take thyself the same provident care for [thy wife] as Christ takes for the Church. Yea, even if it shall be needful for thee to give thy life for her, yea, and to be cut to pieces ten thousand times, yea, and to endure and undergo any suffering whatever—refuse it not. Though thou shouldst undergo all this, yet will thou not, no not even then, have done anything like Christ.

Shamed

Paul's heady challenge also serves to shame me. For above my desk, facing me every day I come to work, is the little prayer I've written down from Gordon MacDonald: "Lord, above all the things you allow me to be and to do, make me a good husband and an effective father. For, by contrast, nothing else much counts."

I feel so ashamed. How often I fail to put my prayer into practice and to turn these words into actual deeds of love toward my wife. Continually I must pray the medieval monk's prayer: "O Christ, who lovest me, set my own loves in order."

Awestruck

Paul says, further, that husbands "ought to love their wives as their own bodies" (5:28). "After all," husbands and wives are "one flesh" (5:29, 31; Gen. 2:24). Now, the Greek words that Paul uses here say literally that a husband "nourishes" and "cherishes" his "body" (including his wife) "just as Christ does the church" (Eph. 5:29). Reminding us here that the church is Christ's body and that we are all members of it (5:30; 1 Cor. 12:12-27), Paul is pointing out that Christ's nourishing and cherishing of the church is a *model* for the husband's relationship with his wife.

In 5:32 Paul reaches a fever-pitch of grand joy and excitement as he describes the gospel's implications for Christians who marry. He says, "This is a profound mystery—but I am talking about Christ and the church." The Greek word for "mystery" here is *musterion,* which, translated into Latin, is *sacramentum* ("sacrament, will, testament"). The word *musterion* itself is a sort of mystery because it's almost untranslatable. It has something of the surprising, the breathtaking, and the captivating to it. A *musterion* is something mysterious—you could never have dreamed up the idea on your own. In this sense, a *musterion* is arresting, grace-filled, and, because it issues from God, it's full of astonishment and wonder.

But *musterion* also has a kind of "stands-for" quality to it. Each *musterion* (*sacramentum*) "re-presents" visibly something beyond it that, although very real and powerful, is nonetheless invisible and beyond human ability to know fully. To be sure, the "re-presentation" (the *musterion)* is only a faint approximation of what it "re-presents," but it, too, is powerful and real.

Take the Christian sacraments of baptism and the Lord's Supper, for example. They "re-present"—make visible and tangible—something that in essence is beyond mortal sight and touch. In one sense, the elements used are so plain and ordinary—water, bread, grape juice. But in quite another sense these elements are anything but ordinary. Used sacramentally, they come to "sign-ify," to "re-present" Christ to us.

A Christian marriage lived out carefully and faithfully by its partners is a *musterion,* says Paul. And both senses of the word apply. First, the institution of marriage itself has something of wonder, surprise, and grace to it. Who but God in his ever-surprising goodness and grace would ever have thought of calling something like marriage into existence and maintaining it for us humans to enjoy?

But a Christian marriage also "re-presents." It has a "stands-for," show-and-tell quality. Take a long, careful look at what goes on between a Christian husband and wife while they, in imitation and honor of their Lord, day by day try to keep their vows to love each other and to submit to each other. When you're finished, you'll be led to say, "How like

Christ this all really is! Their relationship reminds me of Christ's relationship toward his people, the church. These marriage partners really do try to forgive each other, just as God has forgiven them! What's more, how like God they are in their unswerving commitment to each other!"

Conclusion

Marriage is taking a hit nowadays. What once seemed to be nailed down as sure and lasting in our culture is coming loose. Our generation's conversation is sprinkled far too often with "As long as she/he pleases me" and far too seldom with "Till death do us part." The twin bulwarks of marriage—commitment and self-giving love—are gradually eroding.

God, however, continues to call us toward something better. Still today our Lord implores wives, "Submit to your husbands." And to husbands comes the divine command "Love your wives." Both of these commands saw against the grain of our sinful, selfish tendencies.

And so they should. For both tend toward living within a marriage relationship as God intends—fruitfully, with fulfillment, and with solid joy.

General Discussion

1. How would you compare the cultural pattern for marriage in North America today (also among Christians) with the pattern that prevailed in the days of Paul? What's the same? What's different?
2. In *God's New Society,* a commentary on Ephesians, John Stott writes, "As for the wife's duty in the marriage relationship, it surprises me how unpopular this passage is among many women. When it is read at a wedding and it provokes a feminine outcry, I find myself wondering how carefully it has been read and in particular whether it has been read in its total context." How do you respond to Stott's observation? Would you find it inappropriate for a bride to include in her wedding vow the promise "to obey" her husband? Explain.
3. Respond to the following statement: "With his notion of male 'headship' in marriage, it's obvious that Paul simply bought into the male-dominated, patriarchal system of the ancient world."
4. The study-guide notes (above) say that Ephesians 5:21 presents "the fundamental pattern that ought to prevail among Christians." How does (or should) the rule of mutual submission work itself out in a Christian marriage? How does this rule fit with the instructions that follow in Ephesians 5?

Ideas for Small Groups

Opening (5-10 minutes)

Pray—Open your meeting with prayer, asking God for wisdom and insight as you study about submitting to each other "out of reverence for Christ" (Eph. 5:21).

Share—Share how you're doing on your goals from previous lessons, and report on any group projects you may be doing.

Focus—Keep in mind the following question as you work through this lesson: *What is God saying to me in Ephesians 5:21-33?*

Growing (35-50 minutes)

Read (Optional)

As a group, you may want to read the Scripture passage together (as well as the study-guide notes) before moving into your discussion time.

Discuss

Before choosing from the following process questions, try working through most or all of the "General Discussion" questions, if you have enough time.

On submitting to each other in love:

- In this lesson, have you learned anything about Ephesians 5:21-33 that you hadn't known before? Anything that surprised you? Explain.
- Whether you're a wife, a husband, or single, in what ways would you like to apply the teachings of this Bible passage to your own life? To your relationships with others?
- What do these teachings about husbands and wives, Christ and the church, tell you about unity? In what ways do you see these teachings guarding believers against evil?

Goalsetting (5 minutes)

Try working on the following goal in the coming week:

- Here's how I'd like to apply to my life what I've learned in this lesson, with the help of Christ and his Spirit:

Closing (5-10 minutes)

Preparing for Prayer

Share items that you'd like the others in your group to bring to God in prayer for you. Mention praises and concerns, goals you've made during this Bible study, and so on. You may also wish to read the following statement from *Our World Belongs to God* (st. 47):

Since God made us male and female in his image,
one sex may not look down on the other,
nor should we flaunt or exploit our sexuality.
Our roles as men and women must conform
to God's gifts and commands
as we shape our cultural patterns.
Sexuality is disordered in our fallen world;
grief and loneliness are the result;
but Christ's renewing work gives hope
for order and healing
and surrounds suffering persons
with a passionate community.

Prayer

Close your meeting with prayer, asking Christ to help you live together in love for his sake, ever looking to God for guidance, ever remembering Christ's own example of self-sacrificing love. Everyone may join in with their prayer concerns and praises. Encourage each other to work hard at the goals you've set during this and other sessions. Before leaving, you may wish to sing together the old favorite "Blest Be the Tie That Binds," or another song that focuses on unity in the body of Christ and our mutual care for each other in living for Jesus.

Group Study Project (Optional)

Some or all of you may wish to learn more about "the headship issue," which often comes up in matters related to men, women, and church government. Find out about your church's position on this issue and how it has arrived at that position. Or learn about the positions or perspectives of various other churches. If you like, for the sake of comparison, you might also gather information from sociological and psychological texts about church and household matters. Contact your local church leaders, church and community libraries, denominational offices, bookstores, and so on to see what you can find. If you have time, try to report back on this topic during your next session, which focuses again on household relationships.

12 Parents and Children, Masters and Slaves

Ephesians 6:1-9

[1]Children, obey your parents in the Lord, for this is right. [2]"Honor your father and mother"—which is the first commandment with a promise—[3]"that it may go well with you and that you may enjoy long life on the earth."

[4]Fathers, do not exasperate your children; instead, bring them up in the training and instruction of the Lord.

[5]Slaves, obey your earthly masters with respect and fear, and with sincerity of heart, just as you would obey Christ. [6]Obey them not only to win their favor when their eye is on you, but like slaves of Christ, doing the will of God from your heart. [7]Serve wholeheartedly, as if you were serving the Lord, not men, [8]because you know that the Lord will reward everyone for whatever good he does, whether he is slave or free.

[9]And masters, treat your slaves in the same way. Do not threaten them, since you know that he who is both their Master and yours is in heaven, and there is no favoritism with him.

In Ephesians 6:1-9 Paul continues his discussion of how Christian believers, having submitted to Jesus as their Lord, are now also to submit to one another (Eph. 5:21). Children have new duties toward their parents, and parents toward their children (6:1-4). Slaves, too, must adopt a new attitude and posture of obedience toward their masters; masters, in turn, must relate properly to their slaves. All of this comes into effect because Christ reigns as Lord of all.

Parents and Children

If you had asked me, before I became a parent, whether I thought child-rearing were difficult or easy, I would have said, "Not too hard." After all, I was an expert: I had taken "Marriage and the Family 101" in college.

Then I became a father.

Having become parents, Marcia and I gradually discovered that each of our children is infinitely complex; the very moment we think we've got them figured out, they catch us off-guard and take us by surprise. Bringing them up is by no means a piece of cake. Even under the best of circumstances—good parents, sweet children—child-rearing is pretty tough business. For there's often a great difference between how parents and children *ought to* relate and how they really *do* relate.

As God intended families to function, parents serve as God's accomplices. Children are his blessing to them—not nuisances, as many people in today's society consider them. Scripture calls children "a heritage from the LORD" (Ps. 127:3).

Parents are to teach their offspring diligently (Deut. 6:7-8), for through them God intends to transmit his will and ways from one generation to the next. And the family structure is God's favored environment for doing so. Healthy and strong families, then, are precious and important—to parents, to their children, and, finally and preeminently, to God himself.

Within the Christian economy, the status of children too—like the status of women—took a giant leap forward from what it had been. Once Christ appeared, their position became safer and more protected.

Among the pagan Romans, children were anything but safe. A Roman father held absolute sway. His *patria potestas* guaranteed him the right to enslave them, to tyrannize them, to punish them mercilessly, even to sell them if he wished.

William Barclay notes, "Further, the power of the Roman fathers extended over the child's whole life, as long as the father lived. A Roman son never came of age."

With relationships between fathers and their children in the ancient world so sadly deteriorated, the gospel of Jesus Christ burst onto the scene with vital energy. It called for children to be good toward their fathers, obeying and honoring them—but also for fathers to love their children, not exasperating or embittering them.

A child's duty toward parents is twofold: to obey (*hypakouete*), an act of submission; and to honor (*tima*), an attitude of respect (Eph. 6:1-2). Parents serve as God's functionaries toward children, and "through them God chooses to rule us," as the Heidelberg Catechism says (Q&A 104). Further, to obey is "right" (Eph. 6:1). Here Paul uses the word *dikaion,* a term that indicates that obeying is anchored in the very law of nature itself. For children to obey parents is a precept embedded in the fibers of creation—it is simply right and fitting.

What's more, Paul's mention of "the first commandment with a promise" (6:2) reminds us that obedience is also anchored in God's specific law to his chosen people. Any of Paul's early readers who had a Jewish background would recognize the familiar words of this promise—"that it may go well with you . . ."—which often accompanied Moses' reminders that God must be obeyed (Deut. 5:16; 6:3; 6:18). In fact, as we see in Deuteronomy 6:18 (also in 12:25, 28), Moses often connected obedience with doing "what is right and good in the LORD's sight, so that it may go well with you. . . ." Paul clearly makes this connection too (Eph. 6:1-2). Further, Deuteronomy 12:25 adds "that it may go well with you and your children after you"; in other words, obedience brings on a chain reaction of blessing that can continue through the generations. Honoring parents—and other authority figures—will bring peace and blessing (*shalom*) to your living, as you, in turn, are honored by your children, and they by theirs. Disobedience, on the other hand, will bring trouble (a curse). In other words, if you fail to honor your parents, your children will also dishonor you, and so on. This connection between obedience/disobedience and its natural consequences (blessings/curses—Deut. 28) would likely come to mind among Paul's Jewish readers also.

Now, if children's duty is to obey, their parents' corresponding duty is obvious: parents must not become slack in calling for obedience from their children. They must be worthy of the honor they require of their children, but parents may never tire in their parental duty of insisting upon that honor. What an important reminder for permissive parents who have surrendered their awesome responsibility!

But parents must do more than insist upon obedience and respect. Never may they exasperate their children, lest they become discouraged (see Col. 3:21). Rather, they must encourage their children always.

How sad it is when parents take it upon themselves to berate their children. Or when a child is so coaxed and prodded by her parents' continual push to do her best that she ends up feeling tired, frustrated, humiliated, and not very worthwhile—not to them, herself, or anyone else. Parents can murder their offspring this way—easily.

Their positive duty as parents is to rear their children in the "training" (*paideia:* "discipline, healthy regimen") and "instruction" (*nouthesia:* "appropriate mindset") of the Lord (Eph. 6:4). Parents' devotion to Christ puts their relationship to their children in a new light. They become serving parents by equipping their children to be the Lord's servants.

To strike a proper balance between warm encouragement and sturdy discipline is hard to do, as any parent knows from experience. How important, therefore, that all parental effort be shaped and guided by a wisdom beyond our own. It must come from no one but the Lord himself (6:4).

Slaves/Masters (Employees/Employers)

Just as the status of women and children improved drastically after Jesus entered the world, so also did the status of slaves. Empowered by the Holy Spirit, both slaves and their masters came to see themselves as belonging to a higher master, the Lord himself. Once they acknowledged this single and revolutionary truth, inevitably they also began, once and for all, to change the way they related to one another. No longer were slaves simply chunks of protoplasm to their masters—mere "living tools," as Aristotle had classified them.

(Varro, another ancient who did not believe in God, claimed he had three classes of agricultural tools: those that could speak, the slaves; those that could bellow, the cattle; and those that were mute, the implements.)

Let's admit it, however: early Christianity did not abolish the institution of slavery. Christian masters kept holding slaves; and Christian slaves, now converted and bonded to Christ, didn't thereby immediately free themselves from their earthly masters. To do so would have torn too violently the sinews that held human society together; it would have brought the people's life together to a too-abrupt and calamitous end. Nothing would have worked any longer, for there were 60 million slaves performing vital service by their manual labor.

What early Christianity did, however, was no less revolutionary than if slavery itself had been abolished by one hard sweep of a broom. It proclaimed that both slaves and their owners belong to Christ, that the earthly rank of each has no final importance in heaven's eyes, and that the heart of each must be properly inclined toward the other. Once hearts become softened and more mellow toward others in society, whomever they might be and whatever their status, then society's organizations, institutions, and systems inevitably also begin to change. They must, for the pressure to change comes from within.

The duties of slaves—and today, of employees—are clear. They must perform their tasks in a very specific manner:

- with *obedience* (*hypakouete*—6:5), doing well what the person in charge requests of them
- with *appropriate respect* (*phobou kai tromou*—6:5) for the authority of the person in charge
- with a *sincere heart* (*haploteti tes kardias*—6:5)—that is, eagerly, and to the best of one's ability
- with *loyalty* (*me kat' opthalmodoulian*—6:6)—that is, not with "eye-service" but, rather, with solid devotion and earnest ambition
- with *vital energy* (*met eunoias*—6:7), with wholehearted eagerness, enthusiastically, as serving the Lord and not merely another human being

Likewise, Paul commands masters, "Treat your slaves in the same way" (6:9). Not that masters are now to yield obedience to their slaves as well as to expect it from them—that would be sheer chaos. Some must give orders, and others must take orders; some must lead, and others must follow. What Paul means here is that masters—and, today, employers—must give those who serve under them their proper and fitting respect. For, together, both masters and slaves, both employers and employees, belong to Jesus.

Conclusion

Recently at Calvin College we invited a prominent and wealthy gentleman to participate in an annual lecture series. Of course, he brought in a full house, for everyone was eager to hear what he had to say on his topic, the mania and magic of professional sports.

The person who introduced our guest praised him to the skies. We welcomed the speaker warmly. He stepped to the podium to speak, and we all hushed. The first words were the most memorable of his entire speech: "Well, thank you for those kind words of introduction. But all that doesn't matter, really. What matters is this: 'I, _____, am just a sinner saved by grace.'"

How true. One's earthly status, whether low or high, is no big deal in the final reckoning of things. For, as the Italian proverb aptly puts it, "When the [chess] game is over, both the king and the pawn wind up in the same box."

Far more important—eternally important—is to know that one belongs to Jesus Christ. John Newton, a former slave-dealer whom Christ so totally set free that he never cargoed and sold others again, sized up his life during his final days. Awestruck by divine grace, he whispered to those around him, "My memory is nearly gone now, but two things

I recall: that I am a great sinner, and that Christ is an even greater Savior."

No matter who we are, no matter what our station in life, "he who is . . . [everyone's] Master . . . is in heaven, and there is no favoritism with him" (6:9). Every one of us is equal before God, for "all have sinned and fall short of the glory of God" and in Christ "all who believe" are made right with God (Rom. 3:22-24).

General Discussion

1. Often we rationalize or excuse the inappropriate or disobedient behavior of our children by saying things like, "That's the way kids are," or "Kids will be kids." Do you think we're more inclined to excuse our children or to hold them accountable as children-disciples of Christ? Are our expectations too high or too low? Explain.
2. Identify at least three concrete ways in which Christian parents (including yourself, if you're a parent) are often guilty of "exasperating" their children. Then identify at least three concrete ways in which Christian parents may raise their children "in the training and instruction of the Lord" (Eph. 6:4).
3. Why does the good news of Jesus Christ ultimately find slavery unacceptable?
4. Read Galatians 3:28 and Colossians 3:11. If Paul said that in God's kingdom there is no more slave or free, why didn't he just call for a radical break from the societal pattern of his day? What purpose could be served by asking Christian slaves to accept their slavery and willingly submit to their masters?
5. What principles in Paul's instructions to slaves and masters can we apply to the North American labor world today (for example, our view of work, responsibility on the job, relationships in the workplace)? What other biblical principles should we apply?

Ideas for Small Groups

Opening (5-10 minutes)

Pray—Open your meeting with prayer, thanking God for the relationships we have in our society and asking the Holy Spirit to help you apply Ephesians 6:1-9 to your daily living for Christ.

Share—Share how you're doing on goals from previous lessons, and touch base on any group projects you may need to report on. *Note:* If any of you gathered information about headship ("Group Study Project," lesson 11), you may wish to share that now or at another time during this session.

Focus—Think about the following question and keep it in mind as you work through this session: *What do I value most in my relationships with others?*

Growing (35-50 minutes)

Read (Optional)

As a group, you may wish to read the Scripture passage (along with the study-guide notes) before moving into your discussion time.

Discuss

Before choosing from the following process questions, try working through the "General Discussion" questions, especially questions 2-5, which focus on parents and children and the workplace.

On parents and children:

- Try to "live into" the passage for this lesson by imagining you're a ten-year-old in Paul's day and you're hearing the letter of Ephesians read in your church for the first time. What's your reaction? Next imagine you're a parent. What's your reaction now?
- In what ways, if any, do you now read the familiar teachings of Ephesians 6:1-4 differently than you used to? (Or if the passage is new to you, what do you think is most memorable about it?)

- What do these teachings tell you about unity in Christ? Potential dangers if you don't follow them?

On today's workplace:

- Reflect on a work-relationship problem that you've had (or know of) in which the problem was resolved. Which of the principles in Ephesians 6:5-9 helped to bring about resolution? What did you learn from the experience?

Goalsetting (5 minutes)

Try working on the following goal in the coming week:

- Here's how I'd like to apply, with Christ's help, what I've learned in this lesson about relating to others:

Closing (5-10 minutes)

Preparing for Prayer

Share items that you'd like the others in your group to bring to God in prayer for you.

Prayer

As you close with prayer, ask the Lord to help each one of you try more and more to show Christ's love in all your relationships, especially with your closest loved ones and fellow workers. Group members may join in with their prayer concerns and praises. Wish each other God's peace and strength as you try to meet the relationship goals you've set for the coming week.

13 Under Attack, Standing Firm

Ephesians 6:10-24

[10]Finally, be strong in the Lord and in his
mighty power. [11]Put on the full armor of
God so that you can take your stand against
the devil's schemes. [12]For our struggle is not
against flesh and blood, but against the
rulers, against the authorities, against the
powers of this dark world and against the
spiritual forces of evil in the heavenly realms.
[13]Therefore put on the full armor of God, so
that when the day of evil comes, you may be
able to stand your ground, and after you
have done everything, to stand. [14]Stand firm
then, with the belt of truth buckled around
your waist, with the breastplate of righteous-
ness in place, [15]and with your feet fitted with
the readiness that comes from the gospel of
peace. [16]In addition to all this, take up the
shield of faith, with which you can extin-
guish all the flaming arrows of the evil one.
[17]Take the helmet of salvation and the sword
of the Spirit, which is the word of God.
[18]And pray in the Spirit on all occasions with
all kinds of prayers and requests. With this
in mind, be alert and always keep on praying
for all the saints.
[19]Pray also for me, that whenever I open
my mouth, words may be given me so that I
will fearlessly make known the mystery of
the gospel, [20]for which I am an ambassador
in chains. Pray that I may declare it
fearlessly, as I should.
[21]Tychicus, the dear brother and faithful
servant in the Lord, will tell you everything,
so that you also may know how I am and
what I am doing. [22]I am sending him to you
for this very purpose, that you may know
how we are, and that he may encourage you.
[23]Peace to the brothers, and love with
faith from God the Father and the Lord
Jesus Christ. [24]Grace to all who love our
Lord Jesus Christ with an undying love.

No doubt about it: this world is no friend to God's people. No matter where and when God calls us to follow in fellowship and obedience, there Satan is sure to counter-call—and to fight savagely.

The Devil at Battle

Satan waged heavy war even against Jesus. At the beginning of Jesus' ministry, Satan tempted him for forty days (Luke 4:2). And to the very end, the devil kept up his relentless attack: while Jesus writhed in agony on the cross, willingly and obediently taking upon himself the world's entire evil, he heard Satan scream, "Come on down if you're the Son of God!" (see Matt. 27:40).

The devil's battle raged against every one of Jesus' earliest followers too. Take Paul, for example. Rehearsing the record of troubles he faced, he says, "Five times I received from the Jews the forty lashes minus one. Three times I was beaten with rods, once I was stoned, three times I was shipwrecked, I spent a night and a day in the open sea . . ."—on and on he goes, recalling the devil-inspired roadblocks and hardships he had to endure (2 Cor. 11:24-28).

At one point during his ministry Paul desired fervently to visit his spiritually infant friends in Thessalonica. "But," he said laconically, "Satan stopped us" (1 Thess. 2:18). No Christian (or group of Christians) should ever expect to be handled any differently by their archenemy, the devil. Paul warned the elders of Ephesus, "I know that after I leave, savage wolves will come in among you and will not spare the flock" (Acts 20:29). And to Timothy he wrote, "Everyone who wants to live a godly life in Christ Jesus will be persecuted" (2 Tim. 3:12).

Satan's clever strategy of assault can vary widely. Paul spoke of being given a thorn in his flesh, "a messenger of Satan," to torment him (2 Cor. 12:7). But since Paul didn't go into detail, no one today knows the exact nature of the trouble. The evil one will set upon a believer with utterly devious and mischievous schemes, hoping to keep that Christ-follower from knowing and living by the promises and commands of God and from experiencing firsthand the grandeur of God's *shalom.* The devil is pesky, persistent, sinister, and complex in his fascinating enticements.

Not for Wimps

The Christian life, therefore, is not for wimps. Take Jesus' way, and know that you're going to be in for a fight. Time and again, Scripture summons up battle metaphors to describe the circumstances we believers are in. Spiritual opposition surrounds us (Phil. 1:27-30). So we must always be on guard and "fight the good fight" (1 Tim. 6:12). While at "war" with evil influences deep within us (Rom. 7:23), we are to "stand firm" (Eph. 6:14), for the devil is "filled with fury" (Rev. 12:12). Well aware of the devil's tenacious, wily, deceiving ways, Paul encourages his readers, "Be strong in the Lord and in his mighty power" (Eph. 6:10).

Scripture's call to arms is an urgent summons never to take evil lightly but to be deliberate in resisting it. We'll never lick our wicked opponent and become victorious without being alert and intentional. A person may wander his way into hell, but a person will never lolligag his way into heaven.

The wicked opponent we face is stronger than we are. And he's as crafty in his wicked fury as he is strong. "For our struggle is not against flesh and blood, but against the rulers, against the authorities, against the powers of this dark world and against the spiritual forces of evil in the heavenly realms" (6:12). Sinister and supernaturally powerful, the devil's legions oppose us all.

No amount of personal goodness we possess, no human ingenuity or savvy, however great, will ever be able to lick our spiritual enemies. We need daily, hourly, even minute-by-minute resistance. And we have that only when we are "strong in the Lord" (6:10); our full reliance and confidence for victory must reside in no one but the one God who saves and recreates us in Christ. For only in God's power can we stand against "the spiritual forces of evil." Paul calls us, then, to "put on the full armor of God" (6:11, 13). We must become skilled at putting on and using several instruments that can protect us spiritually and can help us fight against our opponent. These instruments are the spiritual disciplines.

"Put on the Full Armor"

Paul urges us to buckle up with *"the belt of truth"* (6:14). Standard military issue for every Roman soldier was a wide leather belt. When tightened, it both tucked in his garments and held his sword. The belt made him ready for the fight. Without it, a soldier would trip all over himself and stumble in his own battle dress.

Jesus knew how important truth is to our Christian struggle. He prayed, "Sanctify them by the truth; your word is truth" (John 17:17)—and by this he means a thorough knowledge of the teachings (doctrines) of biblical Christianity.

But are we aware of how important truth is? We live in a relativistic era of "You believe your way, and I'll believe my way." Truth, our age stupidly supposes, no longer much matters. But without tightening around our waists the deep and enduring truths of God's Word, we'll never be fit for battle. Truth counts, and doctrine matters—a lot.

Next, be sure to have *"the breastplate of righteousness* in place" (Eph. 6:14). "Righteousness," of course, can mean either "Christ's righteousness" accomplished on our behalf, or our own acts of holy and righteous living. Both are necessary for the spiritual fight. As we wrestle the evil one, we must valiantly sing into his face, "My hope is built on nothing less than Jesus' blood and righteousness." We must also do good and be holy, for slovenly living eventually will drift us away from Jesus, who protects us in the fight.

Our feet must be *"fitted with the readiness that comes from the gospel of peace"* (6:15). Though he doesn't say so, Paul is surely referring to a soldier's footwear, essential gear for keeping a firm, solid footing at all times. Christian soldiers must always be ready and eager to step forward and declare the gospel. "Always be prepared to give an answer to everyone who asks you to give the reason for the hope that you have," says the apostle Peter (1 Pet. 3:15). Indeed, "how beautiful on the mountains are the feet of those who bring good news, who proclaim peace . . ." (Isa. 52:7; Rom. 10:15).

"In addition to all this," says Paul, "take up *the shield of faith*, with which you can extinguish all the flaming arrows of the evil one" (Eph. 6:16). Each Roman soldier, standing shoulder to shoulder with others, carried his *thureos,* a 2½- by 4½-foot wooden shield covered with metal. Together these shields formed a solid front against almost any enemy advance. Faith does that for Christians: their trust and assurance in God unite with those of others to form a solid front against the evil one and to repel his advances.

Also "take the *helmet of salvation*" (6:17). The final defensive piece, the helmet (*perikephalaia*), was designed to ward off dangerous blows to the head from the mighty, two-handed, double-edged sword (*rhomphaia*). Cavalry soldiers would swing those swords at foot soldiers to decapitate them. Satan's goal is to rob believers of the assurance that they belong to Christ and that their hope in him is secure.

The Christian's one offensive weapon is the "sword of the Spirit, which is the word of God" (6:17). Every Roman foot soldier carried his trusted *machaira,* a six- to eighteen-inch knife, and unsheathed it for hand-to-hand combat. It's the only offensive weapon Paul mentions. Equipped with the Bible and trained to use it skillfully in the Spirit, a Christian can win any spiritual battle.

Paul says the Christian's "sword" is the Word of God. It's important to note that Paul uses the term *rhema* and not *logos* here to describe God's Word. *Logos* is a universal, all-encompassing Greek term meaning "speech, reason, discourse, word." *Logos,* in the Greek mind, referred primarily to the foundation of the entire cosmos; *logos* made the cosmos intelligible. In John 1:1, 14 Jesus is referred to as the *logos,* the very organizing center of all creation.

The word *rhema* points to something altogether different. A *rhema* is something specific, not general. A *rhema* is an apt saying, an applicable word, a compelling and convincing reference.

To use Scripture in combat, in *rhema*-like fashion, is to have at hand an entire collection of pithy Scripture sayings applicable to the combat moment. Consider how Jesus, for example, used Scripture. When tempted by the evil one, he pierced Satan through with the words "It is written . . ." (Matt. 4:4, 7, 10).

Satan never goes away simply because we wish him to. He must be frightened into retreat. Only God's sharp, penetrating Word can do that. Seeing it, he'll always flee—if we're skilled at using it properly.

We'll never be fit and skilled at wielding Scripture as our *machaira* unless we practice, practice, practice with it. We must memorize and meditate upon it, study it thoroughly, and apply its truths to our lives. If we don't, we'll be caught without an appropriate *rhema*—a direct and right word from God for the desperate and crucial moment when we need it. In order for God's Word to spring to our mind and lip, we must first give it deep lodging within our heart.

"And Pray . . ."

Although, strictly speaking, Paul does not include prayer as part of the Christian's spiritual weaponry and armor, he does underscore its vital importance here. "Pray in the Spirit on all occasions," he says (Eph. 6:18). The Greek word for the verb "pray" here is really a participle (*proseuchomenoi,* "praying"), which, for a specific reason, has no definite antecedent. In other words, it modifies nothing in particular—and thus it modifies everything. God is teaching us here that this entire business—outfitting ourselves with spiritual armor and then trying to use it—will fail, miserably and predictably, unless we surround ourselves continually with prayer. No fewer than four times Paul mentions a form of "all" in connection with prayer: "pray . . . on *all* occasions, with *all* kinds of prayers . . . *always* . . . for *all* the saints (6:18-20). Finally, Paul requests prayer for himself too, that he "will fearlessly make known the mystery of the gospel" (6:19).

The "mystery" of the gospel is the simply-too-good-to-be-true, utterly surprising nature of the good news of Jesus. Once we begin to realize how unbelievably good that news really is, it fills us with awe and wonder. It takes our breath away.

The good news also swells us with eagerness to tell others. For this is news about eternal matters, and it's far too good to keep to ourselves (6:19).

A Few Closing Remarks

Paul closes this stirring letter with a few personal notes and a benediction. While it's good to tell the good news about eternal matters, it's also fitting to let other believers in the body of Christ "know how we are" (6:22). This sharing with and caring for each other is a necessary part of being a fellowship of believers. Tychicus will tell Paul's readers the necessary information about him, and this "dear brother" will also serve to "encourage" them (6:21-22).

Paul adds encouragement of his own with a three-point benediction: "peace . . . love . . . [and] grace to all who love our Lord Jesus Christ with an undying love" (6:23-24). To his Gentile (as well as Jewish) readers, this reminder of "grace to all" would reinforce the bottom line of the gospel, which has opened the way for all believers to enjoy fellowship together and with God. Only the everlasting love of Christ can unite us "against the spiritual forces of evil" (6:12) that so badly want to divide and conquer us.

General Discussion

1. What does the term "spiritual warfare" mean to you? How do you experience the reality of this warfare in your life?
2. Respond to the following statement by Martyn Lloyd-Jones: "I am certain that one of the main causes of the ill state of the church today is the fact that the devil is being forgotten. All is attributed to us; we have all become so psychological in our attitude and thinking. We are ignorant of this great objective fact, the being, the existence of the devil, the adversary, the accuser, and his 'fiery darts.'"
3. How is prayer related to the "armor of God" and the call to "stand firm"?
4. Paul began the letter of Ephesians with a wonderful rehearsal of the rich blessings that believers enjoy because of their relationship with Christ. Why do you think Paul closes this letter with a section on spiritual battle? Do you see any connection between the beginning and end of the book? What is it? Do you feel inspired by Ephesians 6:10-20? Why or why not?
5. Having studied the book of Ephesians, point out two or three ways in which your understanding of a benediction like the one in 6:23-24 has grown richer.

Ideas for Small Groups

Opening (5-10 minutes)

Pray—Open your meeting with prayer, thanking God for protecting and caring for all of you, and asking for the Spirit's insight as you study about spiritual warfare and reflect on your study of Ephesians.

Share—Share how you're doing on some of your goals and group projects from previous lessons. In this final lesson you may also want to share with each other how your experience of doing this Bible study compares with the expectations you shared in lesson 1.

Focus—Keep in mind the following question as you work through this session: *What does the term* spiritual warfare *mean to me?*

Growing (35-50 minutes)

Read (Optional)

You may wish to read the Scripture passage together (along with the study-guide notes) before beginning your discussion time.

Discuss

Before choosing from the following process questions, be sure to work through most or all of the "General Discussion" questions, which adapt well to the small group setting.

On spiritual warfare and living for Jesus:

- Mention one or two things you've learned in this lesson about "the armor of God." What insights have you gained about spiritual warfare? About uniting against evil?
- Is there a piece of God's armor that you find particularly helpful in your battle with the devil? If so, which one is it and why/how does it help you?
- Is the connection between prayer and God's armor evident in your own life? In the life of your small group? Your church? Explain.
- What have you come across in the Scripture passage for this lesson that motivates you to live (or keep living) faithfully for Jesus? Share with your group one of the items in your list and tell why it's meaningful to you.

Goalsetting (5 minutes)

Try working on the following goal as you finish this Bible study:

- Here's what I'd like to do as a result of this lesson, or, in general, as a result of studying the book of Ephesians:

Closing (5-10 minutes)

Preparing for Prayer

Share items that you'd like the others in your group to bring to God in prayer for you.

Prayer

Ask the Lord to bless you and keep you, to protect you and help you stand firm against the temptations and attacks of the evil one, and to help you apply this study of Ephesians to your daily living for Christ. Everyone may join in with their prayer concerns and praises. In praise of who God is and all that God does for us, you may wish to conclude this Bible study with a reading of Psalm 8 and a rousing song of praise and wonder to God, such as "Amazing Grace," "And Can It Be," or "Love Divine, All Loves Excelling." Wish each other God's strength and peace as you continue to "live a life of love" (5:2) as Christ's united body standing against the devil's attempts to foil God's purposes in this world.

Group Study Project (Optional)

If any of you would like to learn more about spiritual warfare, we recommend the following titles: *The Screwtape Letters* by C. S. Lewis and *Victory Over the Darkness* by Neil T. Anderson. These books are available in Christian bookstores. For a study of angels, read the book *In the Company of Angels: What the Bible Teaches, What You Need to Know* by Andrew J. Bandstra (CRC Publications, 1995). A leader's guide for group study is also available. Call 1-800-333-8300 for more information.

Evaluations

Before you leave, please fill out the evaluation form at the back of this study guide and mail it to the address below. Any suggestions you make will be helpful to us in developing other studies in the *Revelation Series.* Thank you!

Please mail your evaluations to

Revelation Series / Ephesians
CRC Publications
2850 Kalamazoo Ave. SE
Grand Rapids, MI 49560

Evaluation

Background

Size of group:

- ☐ fewer than 5 persons
- ☐ 5-10
- ☐ 10-15
- ☐ more than 15

Age of participants:

- ☐ 20-30
- ☐ 30-45
- ☐ 45-60
- ☐ 60-75 or above

Length of group sessions:

- ☐ under 60 minutes
- ☐ 60-75 minutes
- ☐ 75-90 minutes
- ☐ 90-120 minutes or more

Please check items that describe you:

- ☐ male
- ☐ female
- ☐ ordained or professional church staff person
- ☐ elder or deacon
- ☐ professional teacher
- ☐ church school or catechism teacher (three or more years' experience)
- ☐ trained small-group leader

Study Guide and Group Process

Please check items that describe the material in the study guide:

- ☐ varied
- ☐ monotonous
- ☐ creative
- ☐ dull
- ☐ clear
- ☐ unclear
- ☐ interesting to participants
- ☐ uninteresting to participants
- ☐ too much
- ☐ too little
- ☐ helpful, stimulating
- ☐ not helpful or stimulating
- ☐ overly complex, long
- ☐ appropriate level of difficulty

Please check items that describe the group sessions:

- ☐ lively
- ☐ dull
- ☐ dominated by leader
- ☐ involved most participants
- ☐ relevant to lives of participants
- ☐ irrelevant to lives of participants
- ☐ worthwhile
- ☐ not worthwhile

In general I would rate this material as

- ☐ excellent
- ☐ good
- ☐ fair
- ☐ poor

Leader's Guide and Group Process (for leader only)

Please check items that describe the material provided in the leader's guide:

☐ helpful, stimulating
☐ not helpful or stimulating
☐ overly complex, long
☐ appropriate level of difficulty
☐ clear
☐ unclear

The Bible study in general was true to the Reformed/ Presbyterian tradition.

☐ agree
☐ disagree
☐ not sure

Please check the procedures that worked best for you:

☐ reading of Scripture
☐ reading of study-guide notes
☐ small-group discussions
☐ whole-group discussions
☐ general-discussion questions
☐ focus questions
☐ process questions
☐ goalsetting
☐ group projects
☐ other (please write in)

Additional comments on any aspect of this Bible study:

Name (optional): ____________________
Church: ____________________
City/State/Province: ____________________

Please send completed form to

Revelation Series / Ephesians
CRC Publications
2850 Kalamazoo Ave. SE
Grand Rapids, MI 49560

Thank you!